Paths to School Readiness

Paths to School Readiness

An In-Depth Look at Three Early Childhood Programs

M. Elena Lopez

Mona R. Hochberg

Harvard Family Research Project

Cambridge, Massachusetts

Published by Harvard Family Research Project
Harvard Graduate School of Education
Longfellow Hall, Appian Way
Cambridge, MA 02138

DESIGN AND PRODUCTION: *William R. Brinkley & Associates*
COVER DESIGN: *Scott Wilder*

Library of Congress Catalog Card Number: 93-079081

ISBN 0-9630627-2-7

PRINTED ON RECYCLED PAPER

Contents

Tables

Acknowledgements

To Kathy Brendza of The Center, Linda Cantrell of the Family Services Center and Judie Jerald of Early Education Services for opening their doors to our research activities, and to their staffs who shared with us the trials and joys of family support work;

To Heather B. Weiss for guiding our analysis and sharing her enthusiasm in the preparation of this study;

To Mia MacDonald for her thoughtful reading of our drafts and help in revising the manuscript, and to Tom Schultz for his insightful comments;

To Cecilia Gal, Kate Ouderkirk and Sarah Ng for helping us organize our fieldwork and the voluminous data that we brought back;

To Anya Bernstein, Elaine Replogle and Arlie Woodrum for preparing the appendices of this report and assisting in overall production;

To Penny Bragonier who edited our manuscript, and Katherine Wrean for suggesting its title;

To our families who supported us through the entire project.

This research was funded by the John D. and Catherine T. MacArthur Foundation and the Charles Stewart Mott Foundation. The contents of this publication are solely the responsibility of the Harvard Family Research Project.

I Introduction

American education is taking a new approach to school reform. No longer is it considered sufficient to focus on improvements just within school walls. The circumstances of children's lives today require schools to work closely with the family and the community. Consider the facts:

- One of every five children is poor; one of every seven children is receiving public assistance; and one of every four children is raised by a single parent (National Governors Association, 1992:4).
- One in four children below six years of age grows up in a family that cannot afford safe housing, adequate nutrition, or health care (Boyer, 1991:4).
- One-third of children entering kindergarten lack the skills for school, according to teachers (Boyer, 1991:7).
- Each day 3,000 students drop out of school, as many as one million a year (Cities in Schools, 1991:1).

In 1990, following an education summit, the President and the nation's governors formulated the national school readiness goal. The goal, one of six that were discussed at the meeting, states, "By the year 2000, all children will start school ready to learn" (U.S. Department of Education, Office of Elementary and Secondary Education, June 1991). The objectives of the school readiness goal are:

- All disadvantaged and disabled children will have access to high quality and developmentally appropriate preschool programs that help prepare children for school.
- Every parent in America will be a child's first teacher and will devote time each day to helping his or her preschool child learn;

parents will have access to the training and support they need for this purpose.

- Children will receive the necessary nutrition and health care needed to start school with healthy minds and bodies; the number of low birth weight babies will be significantly reduced through enhanced prenatal health systems.

The readiness goal is a milestone in education reform. Unlike earlier statements of educational objectives, it focuses on children, rather than schools; it refers to total child development, not just academic preparation; it supports parents in their childrearing functions; and it implicitly recognizes that children's school success requires a partnership of families, schools, and communities.

This report is about three school-based programs that promote children's readiness for school by providing comprehensive family support that includes direct or indirect access to education, child care, health, and social services. Learning from their struggles and experiences, we can begin to answer the following questions: How can schools design and participate in comprehensive family support programs? By what means can they establish programs that will lead to the best outcomes for children and their families? What kinds of thinking and networking are required? How can programs recruit qualified staff and what type of management structures are needed? How can resources be effectively utilized?

Ample documentation exists of the need for a family- and community-focused approach to child development and school success. In a review of research on parent contributions to school readiness, Powell (1991) reports that parents', and especially mothers', childrearing beliefs and practices in the early years are related to their children's later school performance. The work of James Coleman (1987; 1991) suggests that children's relationships with the adults in their families and in the community can create a kind of "social capital" that fosters their development and their success in school, provided that these relationships are based on trust and community-wide norms about children's behavior. Recently, Snow and her colleagues (1991:171 ff.) found that even moderate stress in the family has a negative effect on children's literacy development. They also found that communication between children and adults, and between parents and school personnel, enhances children's literacy skills.

Many early childhood programs are beginning to draw on these research findings in the design of their services. They are combining child and family services to make them more accessible to families through community-based institutions and programs. However, there remains a gap in our knowledge about the means by which effective family, school, and community partnerships are formed and sustained. The following questions remain: While it is fashionable in policy circles to advocate for comprehensive services for children, what does it take to create and implement such service programs? How easy or difficult is it to combine multiple services? What are the strengths of these initiatives, and their limitations? How can these efforts be sustained and expanded?

OUR THREE EXEMPLARY PROGRAMS

There are many ways for educational programs to respond to the multiple dimensions of the readiness goal. Although the three programs in our study all provide comprehensive family support, they differ in their means of service delivery. This study looks at these programs as alternative approaches to achieving the school readiness goal. Each program has had to tailor its services to community conditions and to work with locally available expertise. Although schools are not the only sponsors of family support programs, we focus on them because they occupy such a strategic position in the community. No other institution has such extensive access to children. Schools provide a context for their growth that spans the years from childhood through adolescence. A wholesome relationship established between parents and schools in the early years of a child's life can provide the impetus for sustained parent involvement throughout the child's school years.

Because schools are community institutions, their educational function puts them in a position to bring together public and private services and resources to build a system of comprehensive support for children. They are also open to all community members, regardless of their ethnic, economic, or religious background.

Although the primary responsibility of schools is to educate children, schools have historically addressed children's nonacademic needs as well. Programs such as those providing school meals, health care, guidance and counseling services, and referrals to other community services, are part of a range of supports that can enhance students' school performance. Their success provides a philosophical basis for developing comprehensive services for preschool children who, in the absence of such services, will start school at a serious disadvantage with needs that will extend far beyond educational instruction. What will be new for schools in the coming years is the provision of family-focused services that foster a healthy home environment in which both children and parents will have the opportunity to develop their human potential.

Efforts to promote child development require a careful balance of early childhood education and family services. The three programs in our study have struggled successfully to achieve such a balance. The programs—Early Education Services in Brattleboro, Vermont; The Center in Leadville, Colorado; and the Family Services Center in Gainesville, Florida—share the following important characteristics:

- They involve parents, not just children.
- They provide access to formal programs such as health care, housing, and social services.
- They encourage parent-to-parent networks, thus providing the opportunity for informal social support.
- They enhance parenting skills through the provision of information, modeling, and other means appropriate for adult learners.
- They offer sustained, continuous services to families for at least two years of the young child's life.
- They require and reinforce involvement of parent with child, family with school, and school with community.

The three programs are excellent examples of school leadership in the area of family support. Early Education Services works with many families burdened by unemployment and inadequate parenting and job skills. The Center fills a gap in quality child care for low-income, two-earner families. The Family Services Center simplifies a family's process of gaining access to multiple services by housing these services at one site.

Each of these three programs opened its doors to us for a week and was exceedingly generous with its time, ideas, and reflections. The program directors not only gave us their own candid opinions about their programs' achievements, but also provided us free access to staff, parents, and collaborating community agencies. The close-up and, simultaneously, wide-angle look we were afforded enriched our understanding of the programs' goals and their methods for meeting them.

We chose these particular programs, not only because they are model programs that could and should be replicated, but because they differ from each other in terms of geography, economy, population composition, and type of family served, as illustrated in Table 1.

An Agenda for School Action to Meet the Readiness Goal

Implementing a strategy to meet the readiness goal poses a challenge to every school. All aspects of a child's development must be nurtured; consequently, schools will need to develop the activities and styles of interaction that recognize the individual and social contexts of children's

Table I Selected Characteristics of Programs

Program	Geography/ Population Composition	Economy	Employment of program families
Early Education Services	Rural, white	Service industry	Many nonworking parents
The Center	Rural, mostly white with some Hispanic	Shift from mining to tourism industry	Low-income, dual working parents
Family Services Center	Urban, white and African-American	Government and health services	Many nonworking parents

growth and learning (Kagan, 1990: 277; Katz, 1992:4). An agenda for school action to meet the readiness goal might include the following measures:

Creating a system of support for young children that is family-focused, comprehensive, and coordinated. Schools will need to broaden their mission to meet the complex needs of children and families, a task that can be achieved only with community support. The goal in developing a system of care and education for children must be to encourage school-community partnerships that make effective use of existing services and provide the basis for exploring new and better ways to serve young children and their families. For example, schools can house parenting programs; arrange for child developmental screenings, routine check-ups, and dental care with clinics or hospitals; offer on-site employment counseling and training for parents through community colleges; and coordinate with social service agencies for other assistance families may need.

Offering programs to enrich the developmental capacities and promote the health of young children. Good early childhood programs are engaged in "developmentally appropriate practices" that are child-oriented and sensitive to the cultural background and capabilities of each individual child (Bredekamp, 1992). They involve parents in all aspects of child development, providing them information and support. Schools will need to create a preschool environment that encourages not just children's cognitive development but their physical, emotional, and social development as well. Because the state of a child's health affects his or her capacity to learn, services such as health screening, nutrition advice, and immunizations need to be linked to education programs. In addition, schools will need to facilitate the transition of children and parents from early childhood and family support programs to the K–12 system.

Empowering parents in their family functions and as learners and community members. Schools will need to develop the policies, structures, and services that will support parents as their child's first teacher and encourage them to participate in their child's development through the school years. While it is difficult to sustain parent involvement beyond the preschool years, it is essential that schools try to do so, since parents play an ongoing role in their children's academic performance. In addition to fostering their own children's achievement, involved parents also have a positive impact on the quality of the schools in their community (Henderson, cited in Dornbusch and Wood, 1989:87).

Many schools are already implementing programs that strengthen parenting skills, encourage parents to stimulate their child's language development, and foster informal support networks for parents in their caregiving role. Some school programs are two-generational; they not only support parents in their parenting role, but also offer them the opportunity to enhance their language and literacy skills, advance to higher levels of education, and improve their job prospects. However, much innovative work remains to be done to make parents feel welcome in the school setting and to foster the kind of communication that will help them contribute to their children's school success. The mechanisms for providing family support and cultivating parent involvement must be woven into the fabric of the school's standard operation. Otherwise, the partnership with parents exists as a disconnected effort, isolated from its complex moorings.

Developing the human and organizational capacities to deliver family support. Effective family support programs are characterized by flexibility, team-based management, and highly qualified staff (Schorr, 1988). The school system's capacity to provide staff support, training and career development opportunities, and managerial autonomy influences the quality of family support programs. In addition, family support efforts are bolstered by links with other school programs; staff members profit from sharing their expertise and learning from each other's experiences.

Strengthening the financial bases of programmatic efforts. As states and communities begin to combine a range of child and family services in comprehensive programs, concern exists about whether or not such efforts can be sustained. The experience of previous innovative programs augurs that difficulties will arise in securing sufficient and stable funding. Creative strategies that ensure core program funding, tap diverse resources, and experiment with the reallocation of funds or other resources will help to make programs sustainable.

STRUCTURE OF THIS REPORT

This report is intended to provide practitioners in the field of child and family services with useful information on such topics as program design, community collaboration, funding, and staff management. It is also designed as a resource on the most current thinking about family support programs, as that thinking is tested by the experiences of program directors, staff, and participants. The report will help policy makers see how policies are put into practice, what issues arise during their implementation, and what gaps need to be filled by new policies or modifications of existing ones.

The chapters are organized around the five areas that constitute the main components of establishing and running an early childhood education and family support program. These areas are:

- a comprehensive system of education, health, and social services for young children
- a developmentally appropriate early childhood program
- a family support component to strengthen parents' childrearing roles
- a human resource capacity to deliver comprehensive family support services
- a sound financial base to support program operations.

Drawing on case studies of the three programs studied—Early Education Services, The Center, and Family Services Center—each chapter details the workings of family support programs and the factors that facilitate or hinder the program's functioning. Each chapter ends with a set of guidelines for practitioners.

Programs evolve out of local leadership's response to community problems. Tracing the community origins of the three programs in our study, Chapter 2 explores the different paths they took to provide comprehensive family support. Planning a comprehensive program means building networks and coordinating community services. Chapter 3 covers the programs' different strategies for bringing together health, education, and social services for young children and their families. In crafting family-focused programs, efforts must be made to coordinate the activities planned for children with those planned for their parents. Chapter 4 illustrates the range of education, health, and social services to meet the needs of children, and Chapter 5 those of parents.

Developing a program requires an array of resources. Programs need a staff that is caring and creative, as described in Chapter 6. They also need dollars and in-kind contributions to support their operations. Chapter 7 analyzes several innovative funding strategies and their implications. Programs will continue to face challenges as they venture deeper into the unexplored territory of family-focused systems of service delivery. Concluding this report, Chapter 8 highlights the ways states can support local efforts at comprehensive services for children and families, and remove barriers to their more efficient implementation.

Several appendices supplement the main body of the report. The reader may want to gain quick reference to specific features of the programs. Appendices I, II, and III contain detailed information about each of the three programs in a format that highlights milestones in program development and key operations. Appendix IV documents our field methods and data analysis procedures.

2 Pathways to Program Development

One of the reasons we have so many children in so much trouble is because they have seen so little opportunity, so little responsibility and so little community that they literally cannot imagine the kind of life we are calling them to lead. Where there is no vision, the people perish.

President Bill Clinton
Acceptance Speech
1992 Democratic Convention

Family Support Programs: *The Community Context*

Family support programs must respond to the specific needs and conditions of the communities in which they operate, as the three programs in this study have done from the outset. This chapter traces each program's development—within the framework of its community's needs—through the four stages that define an organization's service delivery. These stages delineate progress from a self-contained family support program to a community-wide effort to build a comprehensive system of services for children and families.

Early Education Services (EES) operates in Brattleboro, Vermont, a town with a population of 12,240 (1990 census) in the southeastern corner of the state, close to both the New Hampshire and Massachusetts borders. Ninety-six percent of the residents are white. More than 90 manufacturing companies operate in Brattleboro, making it an important business center. The town's largest employers are in health care, wholesale food distribution, finance, education, and book and paperboard manufacturing (Brattleboro Area Chamber of Commerce, 1992:29).

Windham County (1990 population: 41,588), where Brattleboro is located, has the state's highest number of reported offenses against women and children, as well as the highest use rate for child protective services. During a typical month, 1,000 Brattleboro households (2,500 people) rely on food stamps; in 1990, 33 percent of the town's kindergartners began school educationally "at risk," up from 22 percent in 1980 (Windham County Family Support Program, 1988:2–8). Social and physical isolation (60 percent of the county's population lives in small towns not served by public transportation) means that families generally use social services sporadically, if at all. A significant number of parents never obtain routine preventive health care, either for themselves or for their children. As a result, regular preschool screenings often identify children with significant physical, emotional, or language problems that have never been diagnosed or treated.

The Center is located in Leadville, Colorado, a town of 3,500 people (1990 census) located 105 miles southwest of Denver. Most of the residents are either white (about 74 percent) or Hispanic (24 percent). Leadville is the major town in rural Lake County (1990 population 6,000). In 1981, a severe economic crisis hit the county: the mine that employed almost all the county's workers closed, costing 3,000 people their jobs. The result was out-migration or, for those who remained, employment at low-wage jobs in area ski resorts located thirty to fifty miles from Leadville. These jobs not only pay substantially less than the mine did—many dual-worker families have smaller incomes now than they had when one parent worked at the mine—but they also require weekend and holiday work. Lake County has the highest unemployment rate in the state, and 28 percent of its families are classified as low-income (McCabe, 1992:4). The transition from a middle- to a low-income community has resulted in many socioeconomic problems, including increasing numbers of teen pregnancies and school drop outs, high adult illiteracy, and a rising incidence of drug, alcohol, and child abuse.

The Family Services Center is located in Gainesville, a city of 84,770 (1990 census) in north central Florida that is the Alachua County seat. Gainesville's population is mainly white (77 percent) and African-American (19 percent); people of Hispanic origin constitute less than five percent of the population. The city has a highly visible professional community and is home to the University of Florida and four major hospitals. However, there is also a "hidden population" of poor people, and the city is divided along economic and racial lines. Twenty-five percent of families in Alachua County have incomes below the poverty level (Alachua County Needs Assessment Committee and the United Way, n.d.:4). Many are the working poor who cannot afford basic services, decent housing or adequate health care.

FAMILY SUPPORT PROGRAMS: *Origins and Growth*

Family support programs vary considerably in the paths they take to develop comprehensive services for children and families. Some begin as modest efforts, others as complex community endeavors. One way to illustrate how varied programs are is to examine the series of stages they go through in developing their capacity to serve different populations, expand their goals, offer a range of services, and collaborate with community agencies to achieve common outcomes for children and families. "The stages are a conceptual framework used to describe the range of program possibilities, from simple single service programs to complex, and as yet theoretical, coordinated community-wide systems of support for children and families....The stages (are) steps of program evolution leading to a family support village in the truest sense—where the entire community subscribes to a common set of service ideals" (Harvard Family Research Project, 1993). These stages are described below.

STAGE 1 *Family Support Services*

The program is usually self-contained and offers a single service or serves a very well-defined population. Early Education Services began as a self-contained parenting program (Stage 1), before developing its range of services to the Stage 2 level.

STAGE 2 *Family-focused Services*

The program offers a broader array of services to families than does a Stage 1 program and develops formal links to other community programs. The program focuses, not only on healthy child development, but also on adult development. Efforts are made to meet the comprehensive needs of individuals and families. The Center began with comprehensive daycare services, early childhood education, and parenting programs involving interagency collaboration (Stage 2), and continues to expand its services.

STAGE 3 *Comprehensive Family Services*

The program seeks to provide comprehensive family services and to improve the entire existing service delivery system. A high degree of collaboration exists among different agencies who share accountability for program outcomes. Programs often pool funding and other resources. The Family Services Center began as a Stage 3 program, housing under one roof a range of health, educational, and social services. Its extensive community partnerships move it closer to a Stage 4 type of service delivery.

STAGE 4 *Community-wide Family-focused Services*

Central to initiatives in this stage is the role of community planning and governance. Services and programs at Stage 4 function in much the same way as those at Stage 3, except that there is now a new organizational structure representing the community's shared authority for making policy, setting budgets, and designing service systems. Presently, this model of intervention operates only at the conceptual level, but some states and localities are initiating plans for a reformed service system along these lines.

Family support programs expand over time in order to provide continuous services to participants. This might take the form of starting with a preschool program that then serves children in their younger years; or it might start with a infant and toddler program that continues to serve preschool and then school-aged children. Programs also expand to offer a wider range of services for children and families, which entails greater coordination with community agencies so that the educational, health, and social service needs of participants are met. Finally, school-based early childhood education programs grow in terms of the linkages they develop within the school system, connecting their services to the activities of elementary and secondary schools. The ways in which family support programs become more complex in their service delivery features is summarized in Table 2.

In practice, a program may have components operating at different levels of complexity. It may, for example, be at Stage 1 with regard to the limited population it serves, but at Stage 2 in its service capacity and level of community involvement. There is no one way for programs to move through these stages. Instead, their course is determined by many factors, including the extent of the community services and resources available to them and the commitment of school and other local leadership to early childhood and family support programs. The next section describes the study's three model programs in terms of their stages of program development.

Table 2 **Framework of Program Development**

Service Delivery Features	**Stage 1**	**Stage 2**	**Stage 3**
Population Served	Children within limited age range, or parents and children within limited age range	Children of different ages and their parents; other adults in the community	Children of different ages and their parents; other adults in the community
Services	Well-defined core activities	Diverse core activities; supplementary services provided by other community agencies	Diverse core activities provided by multiple community agencies
Community Involvement	Informal networks with community agencies for recruitment and referrals	More formalized arrangements for referrals and joint services	Joint activities in service delivery
School Involvement	In-kind contributions	Some coordination with other school programs	Extended coordination of program services with school resources and activities

FROM PARENTING PROGRAM TO COMPREHENSIVE CHILD DEVELOPMENT: *Early Education Services in Brattleboro, Vermont*

Early Education Services (EES) is a good example of a program that began as a modest parenting activity, Parents As Teachers (unrelated to the Missouri Parents As Teachers program), and has expanded into an umbrella organization with programs that meet the broader health, social service, and educational needs of families. The evolution of EES is summarized in Table 2.1 (p. 14).

Alarmed by the numbers of children who were not ready for kindergarten, Brattleboro school officials established a Parents As

Table 2.1 The Growth of a Program from Stage 1 to Stage 2

Early Education Services, Brattleboro, Vermont

Stage 1: A self-contained family support service.

Original program	*Services offered*
1987 *	
Parents As Teachers:	Offers a home-based parenting education program open to all families with children from birth to three years old.

Stage 2: An expanded set of services coordinated with community programs.

Additional programs	*Services offered*
1988 ✖	
Early Education Initiative	Creates a preschool program for at-risk children ages three to five.
1989 ✦	
Even Start	Establishes a family literacy program.
Comprehensive Child Development Program	Provides adult and child services in health, education, legal aid, daycare, and social services.
1990 ✖	
Parent-Child Center	Expands Parents As Teachers to cover the entire county.
1991 ✦	
Follow Through	Offers an enriched curriculum and parent involvement in K–3 classrooms.
1992 ✦	
School/Family Partnership Grant	Expands EES services to four new school districts.

Funding Sources: * Town of Brattleboro, ✖ State Funds, ✦ Federal Funds

Teachers (PAT) program in 1987. The program provides home-based parenting sessions, child development classes, parent support groups, and play groups. It is open to families with infants and children up to three years old, and is supported through local tax funds.

PAT program administrators researched federal- and state-level grants that would support their vision of moving beyond a parenting program to addressing the comprehensive needs of children and families. Whereas the PAT program began with only a team of home visitors, EES now coordinates activities with public health nurses, child care providers, psychologists, and other community specialists. What began as a program for infants and toddlers now works with children up to completion of third grade. A home visiting program that was originally peripheral to school activities is now closely linked to the K–12 system. Much of the expansion of the program from PAT to EES can be attributed to Judie Jerald, now EES program director, who, as a school social worker and member of the town's finance committee, has had many years of experience with families and community agencies.

Fueled by its twin goals of serving the many needs of families and providing continuity of services, EES has enlarged its program to promote adult development and family-oriented initiatives, programs which go beyond parenting skills. As Laurie Emel, former Parents As Teachers director, says, "It's harder for parents to be good parents and good teachers and good advocates for their children if their own needs aren't met. If a parent's unemployed, if a family is about to be thrown out of their apartment, if there are health problems, then it's hard to get parents' attention around parenting skills." In 1991, EES served 170 families and 232 children throughout Windham County.

THE SCHOOL AS "EXTENDED FAMILY": *The Center in Leadville, Colorado*

The Center offers family support programs based on providing daycare services. It is an example of a program that began at Stage 2 and is working its way to Stage 3. The original child-oriented focus of The Center has expanded over the years to foster greater parent involvement and provide a variety of community activities, as shown in Table 2.2 (p. 16). The Center began as a school team effort led by Superintendent Jim McCabe, elementary school principal Larry Marriott and early childhood teacher Kathy Brendza. Those three educators convened a group of other educators and daycare and human service providers to discuss ways of addressing interrelated family, school, and community issues. While daycare for dual-worker families was the catalyst for their efforts, they also identified school problems, rooted in community concerns, that called for attention. School screening, for example, indicated that 40 percent of students entering kindergarten did not have the necessary developmental skills to do the work. The school district likewise sought to remedy the failure rate of children from low socioeconomic families and to integrate handicapped children into an early childhood program (McCabe, 1992: 5).

Table 2.2 The Development of a Stage 2 Program
The Center, Leadville, Colorado

Stage 2: An expanded set of services coordinated with community programs.

Children's Programs	
1988	The Center provides childcare, before- and afterschool care, and integration of handicapped children into preschool programs; Lake County Health Department provides health referrals, coordination of developmental screening and primary health care.
1991	Head Start grant provides eligible children with complete physical exam and dental screening.
Parent Programs	
1988	Colorado Mountain College provides on-site parenting classes for new and expectant parents, adult education and English as a Second Language classes.
1991	Head Start grant provides information and referrals to social and mental health services, and parent involvement activities for Head Start parents.
Community Programs	
1991	Office of Substance Abuse Prevention, U.S. Dept. of Health and Human Services, provides Full Circle Intergenerational Project that pairs senior citizens with at-risk youth ages 8–11.
1992	Share Colorado subsidizes food purchase in exchange for volunteer community work.

In 1988, The Center launched simultaneously its high quality daycare, preschool, and before- and afterschool programs. Located in a former elementary school building donated by the school district, it is managed by Brendza. The Center serves as an "extended family" for 600 children of working parents and operates on private sector, federal, and state grant financing. Half of its operational costs are covered by sliding scale fees; parents pay from 50 cents to $1.50 an hour for the children's programs.

In its effort to meet the needs of participating families, The Center has individualized many aspects of its support program. It has, for example, undertaken the Herculean task of transporting children to afterschool sports programs sponsored by other organizations. According to Brendza, "Parents write a schedule where their child is supposed to be....It's a logistical nightmare, but we haven't lost a child yet."

DESIGNING A "ONE-STOP SHOP": *The Family Services Center in Gainesville, Florida*

The collaboration of many community organizations is required to establish a multiservice center. The Family Services Center, an example of a Stage 3 program, developed in response to the high poverty rate and the fragmented nature of existing services for children and families in Alachua County. Superintendent Douglas Magann conceived the idea of school-based services for families and rallied the support of major community agencies to staff a multiservice site. While the Family Services Center cannot necessarily meet all of a family's needs, it does offer a core of education, health, and social services. Some of these services, like health, are open to members of the wider community who are eligible for Medicaid but who are not eligible for the preschool and educational programs at the Family Services Center. Educational activities draw upon a range of school resources, including vocational education, Head Start, and Chapter 1 and Chapter 2 funds.

The Family Services Center, which opened in August 1990, currently serves about 400 families, most of them residing within a five mile radius of the facility. The program is housed in seven mobile units between a middle school and an elementary school on property that the city of Gainesville rents out for a dollar a year. In December 1992, it received $2.5 million from the Florida Department of Education to construct a permanent building. Linda Cantrell, who has a background in school administration and special education, served as program director until July 1992, when she went on leave. The program is now managed by Ann Crowell who has had extensive experience with the Head Start program operated by the school district. Table 2.3 (p. 18) illustrates the course by which the Family Services Center developed its comprehensive program. Notably, it began as a program to serve middle school students, but has since shifted to serve elementary and preschool children. This change is explained further in Chapter 7.

BUILDING COMPREHENSIVE FAMILY SUPPORT PROGRAMS

How do programs develop the means to provide comprehensive family support? How do they manage to bring together the community

Table 2.3 The Expansion of a Stage 3 Program

The Family Services Center, Gainesville, Florida

Stage 3: Extensive collaboration and resource sharing with different service providers creates a system of comprehensive family services.

1990 *Original program*	***Services offered***
School Board of Alachua County	Education and social services for middle school students
University of Florida	Health services for students and families
Alachua County School Board and Santa Fe Community College	Education and counseling for parents
Santa Fe Community College	School-home liaison to facilitate parent involvement in a child's education
Department of Health and Rehabilitative Services	Public assistance for families

1991 *Additional programs*	***Services offered***
STATE FUNDED	
Supplemental School Health Program	Health information, education and counseling for students, families and teachers
Full Service Schools	Health and mental health services, parent involvement activities
Florida First Start	Parenting education for parents of children birth to age three
FEDERALLY FUNDED	
Chapter 2 Parenting Program	Parent involvement activities.
Head Start Family Services Demonstration Project	Support and services for families with problems in the areas of substance abuse, literacy and employability skills
Even Start	Family literacy
Chapter 1, Head Start, Even Start, and Florida Dept. of Education	Adult computer lab funded by these programs and state department

resources required to meet the needs of the families they serve? A striking feature of the three programs in this study is their phenomenal growth over a short period of time (ranging from one to three years). Certain features common to the programs facilitated that growth: community responsiveness, organizational leadership, structural flexibility, sound program design, and service accessibility.

Community Responsiveness

The most successful programs are part of a continuous feedback loop, grounded in sensitivity to the community's needs and a capacity to respond to them. Such programs are, typically, designed by members of the community who bring to the task a broad-based knowledge of local concerns. As primary facilitators of family support programs, school leaders take advantage of the practical knowledge of key players from the community, including: representatives of health, mental health, and social service agencies, daycare providers, and other agencies that work with children. They also invite parents to participate in their discussions.

The Center in Leadville, says Steve Jones, executive director of Leadville's Board of Cooperative Educational Services (BOCES), arose as a local response to local needs, unlike other programs he knows that have been designed by state education administrators and handed to school systems with the directive to make them fit local conditions. Linda Eldridge, assistant school superintendent in Gainesville, remembers the origins of that city's program in a similar way: "The need for the Family Services Center came from the knowledge we had of this community....We were looking for ways to meet the needs of those who were not aware of agencies, their inner workings, and where to get assistance for basic family needs that impact students."

Continued responsiveness to a community's changing needs is as critical to the ongoing success of a program, however, as it is to its inception. Staff in this report's three exemplary programs stay alert to community conditions through their in-house experience, community networking, and records review. They listen to parents' concerns, expressed to them in individual or group meetings. They review formal needs assessments, school data, and census information. Statistical information, alone, can provide a startlingly clear picture of community needs, as, for example, the increase in the number of Brattleboro's children who lack the skills for kindergarten or in the climbing rate of poverty in Alachua County that affects the participants at Gainesville's Family Services Center.

Programs grounded in the community, like the three in this study, adapt to the changing needs of families. While they hold a steady course to meet long-term needs, they also have sufficient flexibility to respond to sudden events or altered circumstances. EES recently organized Family Times, a program of center-based activities for parents and children affected by the state's recession. "Family Times was designed to get families out of their homes to do something fun at a time when many families are having hard economic times and feel somewhat depressed," says Laurie Emel, former director of EES' Parents As Teachers program.

Leadership

School superintendents often play a critical role in guiding the conceptualization and implementation of family support programs. Their office gives them the authority to design new school programs and the clout to influence top community administrators. Leadership, however, need not always come from the top. In Brattleboro, a group of school principals and administrators designed the Parents As Teachers program and then crafted a public relations effort to enlist support for it from town representatives.

At the initiative of the local school superintendents, the service communities in Gainesville and Leadville, respectively, came together to solve problems and design responses to urgent local child and family issues. Douglas Magann, then Gainesville's superintendent, took a bold step in the mid-1980s to integrate education and social services to better serve families. Magann chose to work closely with the Department of Health and Rehabilitative Services (HRS), despite the negative image of this agency in the community, occasioned by controversial child protective services policies. A senior HRS administrator recalls, "We had one superintendent who had gotten educated about social services, really was interested in working with the whole family and not just the student. We've got eleven school superintendents just in this area alone. The rest of them don't feel that way about it. They love being separated from HRS because we are the whipping agency." Over a two- to three-year period, Magann put together a planning team of educators and social service administrators to brainstorm ways of meeting family needs and filling service gaps. The result was the Family Services Center.

As top local administrators in education and social services begin to articulate a shared philosophy about their work with families, barriers to service coordination start to fall. Waivers can be secured to get around restrictive policies and procedures. Linda Eldridge makes this observation, "The obstacles you have to overcome in breaking down the barriers between bureaucracies are such that unless you have the people at the top saying, 'We're going to do this and help you figure out how to do it,' then you're going to be fighting windmills trying to fix problems."

When middle level school administrators initiate a program, they need to cultivate the support of higher level officials. They must communicate effectively with their superiors, encourage dialogue, and share pride in the program's success. Sometimes securing the support of supervisors requires political savvy: This is especially needed whenever program activities stretch the limits of standard operations within a school system. For example, the expansion of Parents As Teachers into the more comprehensive Early Education Services involved the school in helping families meet their needs for economic assistance, employment and training, family counseling, and daycare. The school administration initially resisted the types of expenditures accrued through a federal Comprehensive Child Development Program (CCDP) grant: "This project is doing many things that, as a school, we can't do," one school official said, referring to payments for families' car insurance, dental bills, and enrollment in a weight reduction program.

Although schools frequently offer programs that serve the nonacademic needs of students, they often balk when program directors suggest they provide similar support to students' families. EES director Judie Jerald has done a good job of communicating the importance of family services with the school administration and school board, inviting them to EES meetings, and even taking Brattleboro's new school superintendent to a Washington DC meeting on the CCDP program. That visit convinced the superintendent of the merits of family-focused efforts as an investment in children's school success. Now, as the sponsor of such activities, the school district benefits from local, state, and national recognition of EES as a model family support program.

Flexible Organization

The successful operation of family support programs requires organizational flexibility. Most school-based programs are caught in a bind: They rely on the school system for support and in-kind resources, but they reluctantly labor under the burden of its administrative bureaucracy. The three programs in this study, on the other hand, operate through semi-autonomous structures that give them a comfortable measure of flexibility. This type of organization emerges from a combination of available competent persons to manage the program, and a funding base that is independent of the local school budget. In each case, the programs are beneficiaries of different funding streams or agency collaborations, with the school district functioning as a fiscal agent.

EES, for example, has integrated several state and federally funded programs into a single entity that provides early childhood education and family support. The Center in Leadville operates as a nonprofit organization within the school district. The Family Services Center exists as a separate unit within the school system and has its own principal. The measure of autonomy enjoyed by all three programs, within their individual strategies, allows them many freedoms. They can reach out to preschool children, work intensively with parents, create new projects, collaborate with other community programs, and offer the comprehensive services families need—all of which are new ways of interpreting and implementing the school's mission. In effect, the programs do not have to follow school rules on many of their innovations.

Operating as a semi-independent entity has drawbacks, however. Programs struggle to be recognized as an integral part of their school systems, rather than as just another community program. Of the three programs in our study, the Family Services Center has the closest ties to the public schools. It falls under the early childhood unit of the district, which in turn is part of the division of elementary education. To many in the community, the Family Services Center is legitimated by being managed by a principal—someone automatically recognized as part of the school system. Similarly, the program's teachers in adult education and early childhood belong to the teacher's union; school buses bring parents and children to and from the facility; and the district's program development office scouts for grants and helps prepare the program's proposals. Furthermore, the school administration is trying to connect the Family Services Center with other school programs and resources such as Head Start, vocational education, Chapter 1, and Chapter 2 funded activities. Finally, other principals in the school district—some of whom were skeptical in the beginning—are now thinking about replication in their schools.

Program Design

The most effective family support programs draw on a broad knowledge base when they set out to design new community services. A careful review of the lessons learned by their predecessors and of the attributes of model programs in other states and counties helps identify service gaps and the means by which a new program might fill them. Existing models can serve as the springboard for an innovative approach tailored to the specifics of a local situation.

All three programs in this study have been built on the successes of previous efforts. Parents As Teachers in Brattleboro reflects the school district's commitment to supporting family-based programs. According to Jerald, this family orientation can be traced to the federal Follow Through program implemented in Brattleboro schools in the 1970s. The Follow Through initiative sought to build on gains made by children in Head Start, by providing extra education, social services, health care, nutrition guidance, and medical services to at-risk children through the third grade. Follow Through, says Jerald, "set a stage among educators to look at a program that doesn't go from 8:30 to 3:00, and that involves families." In addition, Jerald looked into the Parents As Teachers program in Missouri and an early intervention program in Yakima, Washington for guidance as she and a committee of school administrators designed the Brattleboro program. Features of the program such as parent involvement in a child's education, home visiting, and center-based support groups were ideas derived from other models; the content of the curriculum and the frequency of home visits were both adapted to meet the needs of Brattleboro's families.

Similarly, The Center in Leadville was influenced by the findings of the Perry Preschool Project in Ypsilanti, Michigan, a 26-year study that was designed to answer the following question: Can high quality early childhood education help improve the lives of low-income children and their families and the quality of life for the community as a whole? The Family Services Center in Gainesville drew inspiration from Head Start's model multiservice approach. In both cases, the new programs enriched and innovated upon the old. The Center adopted the High/Scope child-centered curriculum designed by the Perry Preschool Project, but also integrated classrooms to serve handicapped children and broadened its program to offer health and recreational services for all children. At the Family Services Center, participants are not only referred to programs, but can also receive services such as preventive health care for children on site.

Accessibility

Unquestionably, programs need to be accessible—both physically and psychologically—if they are to be widely used. The features that make a program accessible are dictated by conditions in the community. Various factors influence the decision about whether to offer services in homes or at a center, for example: Are people at work during the day or at home? Do families have transportation? Are people sufficiently motivated to seek services at a center or will the staff need to bring services to their participants?

In rural Windham County, the lack of transportation, the geographic isolation of families, and the reticence of New Englanders to seek help meant that EES staff members needed to go into the homes of participants. The first step was to enroll participants in a home visiting program that offered individualized services. Judie Jerald says, "That special relationship with the home visitor is really a jumping-off place for that individual to grow and develop, and move out into groups. It may take bringing a child to a play group, or mom and dad joining a parent group. After that, parents can become part of a community group in order to become an advocate for something."

Later, Jerald sought and received funds to run a center-based preschool that would provide developmentally appropriate experiences for children whose families could not afford the tuition at private preschools. She then added activity groups where mothers and children could interact with their peers and join community programs designed for group socialization. Jerald found that it is crucial to provide transportation to group activities. She admits, "It's the transportation that makes or breaks you! More than once I've been out driving the van."

Although Leadville is a rural area, like Brattleboro, it was necessary to develop a center-based program to meet the needs of the community's working parents. The program developers knew that there were many very young latchkey children in the area, but it was difficult to get precise information about the problem. People hesitated to admit that their seven-year-old was at home watching the four-year-old without adult supervision. A telephone survey conducted by the school district during the planning stage of The Center showed that 100 children would require daycare and before- and afterschool care. This number grew rapidly, and within four years over 600 children were being served in various capacities. Fortunately, The Center opened in a former elementary school that had ample room for expansion.

In Gainesville, the key planners sought to provide educational, health, and social services in a convenient and holistic way. The long waits and impersonal service at local agencies were causing residents not to seek the help they needed; as a consequence, the well-being of their families was being placed at risk. It was decided that the Gainesville program would co-locate services and use school buses to bring participants to the program; thus, the program met the needs of a segregated urban community with few accessible services and poor public transportation. Parents and children come to the Family Services Center primarily because they need assistance, but also because they experience The Center as a community where people are friendly and caring. As one parent exclaims, "This place is a utopia!"

In addition to being physically accessible, the three programs are also psychologically accessible. Because the programs are school-affiliated and sponsor activities open to all members of the community regardless of income or public assistance status, program participants are spared the stigma that is often associated with visiting a social service agency.

To meet community needs, center-based programs must operate on schedules that are convenient for parents. In order to serve working parents, The Center stays open throughout the year from 5:30 a.m. until 6:30 p.m., even on Thanksgiving and Christmas. It is necessary to be open on holidays because they are the busiest time for the ski resorts where many Leadville parents work. And, in a break with the school calendar, the three programs also operate during the summer, although, in the cases of Brattleboro and Gainesville, on a reduced schedule.

Lessons for Practitioners

The three programs we explore in this report all share five key attributes that are highly correlated with their success: responsiveness to community needs; visionary and risk-taking leadership; the provision of services, informed by past experience, that meets community needs; organizational flexibility; and service accessibility. Here are some concrete guidelines for building these features into a program:

1. *Know your community and design a program around its needs.* This recommendation is first on the list for a reason. Without understanding the needs of a community, service providers cannot plan a useful program. All means possible must be employed to determine community needs: census data, needs assessment surveys, and social service information, as well as discussions with a cross-section of local residents. The best way to determine what methods of service delivery will be most effective is to talk with those who are likely to use the services. Research that is essential in the developmental stage is also critical to the life of the programs as an ongoing process. A continuous effort must be made to keep abreast of changes in the community and to adapt services to meet the community's changing needs. To this end, participants should be periodically solicited for their opinions, either in focus groups or anonymous surveys.

2. *Take the lead in raising consciousness about children and families.* While staying attuned to the day-to-day issues of program management, a good family support center leader also needs to cultivate a long-term vision of how the program will evolve. Family support programs are not easy to establish or sustain. Those who direct their course need to be entrepreneurs in securing funds, risk takers in implementing school reform, and coordinators in attracting community

support. However such leaders must also be willing to delegate responsibility, give credit to others, and allow staff a good deal of discretion. As crucial as an individual in a leadership position may be, a program will succeed only if the community and staff share the sense of ownership.

3. *Create units with the autonomy and flexibility necessary to develop new family support programs within an established bureaucracy.* This type of arrangement can be established by hiring an experienced administrator within the school system to manage the program, pooling together separate programs that nonetheless share similar goals, and finding the start-up funds to support the new unit. Such an arrangement minimizes the red tape of large agencies and enables programs to rapidly expand their community outreach and service provision. It gives program directors a hand in hiring and training staff who are best qualified to deliver family support services. However, lest these programs slide to the periphery of the school system, efforts should be made to vest them with the status, symbols, and share of resources that are part of school culture.

4. *In designing a program, build on the research and knowledge base related to family support services.* Avoid the two extreme approaches to program design: Neither start from scratch nor simply adopt a program that has been successful elsewhere. The wide middle ground requires learning about and, perhaps, even visiting other programs, finding out what works and what doesn't, and then determining what will work in a particular community. Program directors do not have to like a program in its entirety to replicate some of its important features. Picking and choosing from among the best features of many programs, and looking for those that will be most responsive to the needs of a particular community enable program directors to build a successful program. Bringing together individuals from diverse segments of the community, including parents, to brainstorm ideas about what the program should do and how it should do it is a good way to encourage community involvement in the planning stages. Both thinkers who can conceptualize the issues and doers of the community who can transform those ideas into action are needed for successful program design.

5. *Make programs accessible.* Do not assume that, if a program offers exceptional services, people can necessarily overcome transportation obstacles or rearrange their work hours to get to it. If possible, locate a program near frequently-running mass transit or accept the fact that a good portion of program funds must be used to provide transportation. Think about which services can be delivered at the

participants' homes or in satellite centers close to where participants work, live, or attend school. If many participants are employed, make certain that services are available during hours when they are free. Finally, care and consideration need to be given to the name and sponsorship of the program so that it is viewed favorably by potential participants.

3 Working Cooperatively for Children and Families

Collaboration is too important a concept to be trivialized. It must represent more than the shifting of boxes on an agency organizational chart.

Charles Bruner (1991:26)

A strong commitment to families guides the policies and services of all three programs in this study. They share common goals: to make families self-sufficient; to empower parents in their own lives and in their children's education; and to prepare children to be successful students and citizens. However, the goals of these programs extend beyond concrete events, such as getting a Graduate Equivalency Diploma or a job, into the realm of immeasurable life-enhancing qualities. One program's early childhood specialist talks about "bringing out the child's loveable character...so that when they get to kindergarten, and when they get into the school system, someone will like them, even though they may misbehave." Another staff person talks about the process of "empowering adults and children in terms of greater self-esteem, more ability to protect one's self, greater ability to advocate for one's self in the world." The goals of the families served by these programs are multiple and complex, and exceed the resources of any one agency. Therefore, in order to help meet them, the staff of each program collaborates with other community agencies to provide families with comprehensive support.

Strategies for Comprehensive Family Support

Comprehensive family support can be provided in different ways that usually involve a core of direct services supplemented by linkages to other community programs. Each of the three programs adopts a multiple strategy approach, relying on extensive use of referrals, contractual services, coordination, and case management. By leveraging existing resources, family support programs can provide a wide array of services without overspending their organizational budgets.

Referrals: More than Just a Telephone Number

Referrals are the most common mechanism for extending services beyond what a family support program can provide in-house. The effectiveness of referrals depends on the extent to which program managers and staff from different agencies communicate and network with each other. The staff of EES finds it important to know how the agencies with which they collaborate, particularly the public bureaucracies, are structured, and what the functions and procedures of their various units are. This information helps them connect families more efficiently to the appropriate services of these agencies and the processes

Table 3 **Collaborative Strategies of Each Program**

	Program		
Collaborative Strategy	*Early Education Services*	*The Center*	*Family Services Center*
Referrals to other agencies	✓	✓	✓
Referrals from other agencies	✓	✓	✓
Contracted services	✓	✓	✓
Coordinating services	✓	✓	✓
Case management	✓		✓
Co-locating services		✓	✓

involved in obtaining such services. When they make contacts with these agencies, EES staff follow them up with reminders, encouragement, expressions of appreciation, and feedback on the progress of a family mutually served. All this takes time and energy. But without such outreach efforts, staffers at other agencies might lose sight of EES' work, or confuse it with that of other programs—to the detriment of the participating families.

Developing a good system of referrals involves more than telling parents where to go for help. Parents often need information and support from program staff before they can deal with the social service system. "You can't chop people up into little pieces and expect them to trot around from place to place and really hold it all together. It just doesn't happen that way," says Ann Darling, an EES social worker. EES home visitors often act as intermediaries between families and the service systems. Aware that families can be discouraged by bureaucratic behavior, they try to ensure that they will receive personalized treatment. For example, with a participant's consent, home visitors call an agency to which they are referring that person—especially in a crisis situation—and provide background information on the family's circumstances. This kind of advance work increases the likelihood that families will be treated with a little more understanding and less indifference.

Contracting Services: An Opportunity to Expand Family Services

Contracted services are formalized arrangements where agencies, for a fee, undertake training, service delivery, evaluation, or other operations for another organization. Some programs that have the capacity to offer a direct service still choose to contract with other agencies to avoid duplication and to optimize the use of community services. Take the case of EES, which is situated in a town with many resources for family support. EES contracts with other agencies to provide educational tutoring for adults and technical assistance on child care. EES' separate programs may also contract for services from each other. Parents As Teachers (PAT), which was EES' original program and currently the one with the least funding, is a frequent beneficiary of this kind of arrangement. Even Start and the Comprehensive Child Development Program (CCDP)-funded Windham County Family Support Program, for example, contract with Parents As Teachers to provide families with home visits and enroll children in its preschool. The contracts expand PAT's resource base and program capacity.

When programs lack the staff to perform certain direct services, contracting with other agencies is a good, cost-effective solution. In some cases, family support center directors may not have the expertise to manage certain professionals, such as nurses and clinical psychologists. In other cases, they may need services only on a part-time basis or may lack the funds for a full-time position. Contracting under such circumstances makes sense. At the Family Services Center some specialized staff positions, funded by grants to the center, are contracted on a part-time basis from local service agencies. A psychologist from Mental Health Services—a private, nonprofit agency—and a nurse practitioner from the University of Florida, work at the Family Services Center under such an arrangement. The position of a part-time nurse practitioner, "the backbone of the clinic," is funded by the state's Full Service School grant. But, because of liability issues, the program does not hire the nurse practitioner directly; instead, it contracts with the University of Florida's College of Nursing. The college receives the grant money and hires the nurse practitioner, who is then assigned to the Family Services Center.

Coordinating Services: A Bridge to Link Programs for Children and Families

The coordination of complementary services by related agencies results in more efficient service delivery to families. Interagency arrangements can be made on a formal or informal basis and do not involve interagency fees for service. The Center in Leadville has arranged for many outside services to be provided at its facility as a convenience for children and their parents. The public health department, for example, sends staff to The Center on call. During their routine visits, its workers conduct lice inspections and identify children who need immunizations and physical check-ups. They also participate in The Center's inservice training for the infant-toddler program. The social services department rents office space at The Center so that it can provide child and family counseling in a neutral setting and, thus, spare participants the label "troubled family," often attached to those who visit a social service agency office. Colorado Mountain College offers several programs at The Center: a young mothers program which teaches parenting skills to new mothers; a training program for baby-sitters; a life skills class for adults; and preparation for the GED exam (McCabe, 1992:15).

Case Management

Case management is a vehicle for coordinating the services provided to a family by different agencies and involves a lead agency to oversee the process. At group meetings, each agency informs participating members of the range of services a family receives and, thus, can work with the other agencies to avoid service duplication or to develop interventions for new problems that arise. According to Dot Marsden, first director of Parents As Teachers, "PAT ended up quite often being the agency that called other agencies together, because we knew three other agencies were working with a family and we wanted to make sure that we weren't overlapping." Every six weeks agency representatives working with the same families would meet to discuss goals and objectives and make sure they were working in tandem. This early sensitivity to the need to work in a complementary, non-duplicate fashion continued as PAT expanded into EES.

Agencies sometimes differ in their philosophical approach to service delivery; such differences can create problems in case management. The Windham County Family Support Program of EES, for example, adopts a family-focused approach that includes both parents and children. It offers intensive services for sixty families through an interdisciplinary team that deals with multiple family issues. By contrast, other community agencies in the county tend to focus on the individual, rather than the family, and work on single rather than multiple issues. These agencies typically assign individual staff members to address those issues. When the various agencies first started holding case-management meetings, the Windham County Family Support Program sent a team of representatives, while the other agencies sent only one representative each. The other agencies were puzzled by, if not uncomfortable with, the heavy EES presence. EES team members realized that their intensive service model could be daunting, especially to state agency staffers whose work is compartmentalized in traditional fashion and who are burdened with heavy case loads. Subsequently, EES decided to send only one person to represent the Windham County Family Support Program team.

Integrating Services

Several programs will sometimes merge into a single organization as a way of resolving intractable administrative problems. What is the best way to blend parallel or related services in such cases? EES is an example of an umbrella organization that was created to coordinate diverse family support activities administered by the school district. The Center in Leadville was established to consolidate children's services provided by other organizations that lacked the resources or facilities to support them. These services included a daycare center from Colorado Mountain College and a preschool for handicapped children from Mountain Valley Development Center.

Co-locating Services

Locating representatives from several agencies at one site makes their services far more accessible to families. The mechanics of reassignment require smooth interagency networking and agreements to contribute staff support. Since the Family Services Center was established through a joint effort of the school district and the Department of Health and Rehabilitative Services (HRS), assignment of staff from these two entities to work at the Family Services Center was a straightforward exchange: Teaching and clerical support staff are provided by the school district, and HRS assigns a public assistance specialist to the Family Services Center to determine eligibility and process applications for economic assistance. Through coordination and contractual arrangements, other agency partners such as Santa Fe Community College, the University of Florida, and Mental Health Services assign their staff to the Family Services Center, rounding out the education and health services offered on site.

The Family Services Center is located in the area of Gainesville that has the highest concentration of families served by the major collaboration partners, the school, and HRS. In order for co-location of services to make sense in economic and administrative terms, a crucial consideration in designing the Family Services Center was its accessibility to a large pool of eligible families. It was important to have sufficient numbers so that outposting staff would be efficient for agencies that have large caseloads.

COLLABORATION ISSUES: *Strategies for Managing Conflicts*

Community-based, collaborative efforts are needed to create the nurturing environments that support children and help prevent such problems as lack of school readiness and school failure. The three programs in our study are models of collaboration, as defined by Benard (1989:71): "Collaboration is a relational system of individuals within groups in which they share mutual aspirations and a common conceptual framework; and their interactions are characterized by a consciousness of, caring for, and commitment to work with others over time." However, collaboration raises many important issues that program planners and directors have to deal with in order to maintain and expand their programs. Some of the issues that the three programs have confronted are turf conflicts, equity concerns, the management of co-located staff, and the cultivation of productive interagency partnerships. Each of these is summarized in the textbox and explained below.

Managing Turf Conflicts

COLLABORATION ISSUES

- Establishing effective communication among agencies
- Avoiding service duplication
- Defining roles and responsibilities for all collaborating agencies
- Ensuring resource equity among agencies
- Managing co-located staff
- Sharing leadership
- Negotiating philosophical differences among agencies

Turf conflicts can develop when overlapping services compete for the same resources or client populations. Good communication, shared decision making, and reciprocity are strategies used by the three programs to garner the community support that was valuable in preempting or defusing such conflict. The relationship The Center established with Leadville's home daycare providers is a case in point. The Center was a high quality, low-cost competitor for daycare services. Home daycare providers were, first of all, invited to participate in the planning of The Center. Later, The Center began to train and, subsequently, employ providers whose businesses suffered from competition with its own, higher quality program. At the same time, The Center offers back-up services to those providers who have sustained their home-based operations; if a service provider is ill or faces an emergency, for example, The Center temporarily makes room for her charges in its own daycare program. Local school officials credit The Center with significantly upgrading the town's child care services.

Effectively communicating an agency's goals and roles can also ease tension in the service community. EES adopted several strategies when rumors circulated that it would use grants from several federal sources to push private agencies out of business. Jerald and key EES administrators met with agency directors individually and held group meetings to clarify the organization's goals and the ways it wanted to work with community service providers. Jerald says, "We deal with criticism by being upfront and honest and doing the best we can."

One way programs can avoid turf conflicts is by providing a service that is clearly distinct from those that already exist. In Brattleboro, the administrators of service agencies became concerned that the CCDP grant to EES would duplicate and compete with existing programs. "Do not duplicate any service that's being provided," one public agency administrator told Jerald. "You can have a model project, but you do not provide everything. Everyone needs to get credit for what it is they provide." Therefore, the staff at EES sought to identify an activity that would differentiate EES from other programs serving young children and their families and would complement the existing services. They chose to claim an intense home visiting program as their niche. Other agencies have, subsequently, come to value this program as a vehicle for reaching families with information about the services they offer, such as dental care, and treatment for substance abuse. Jerald says she "bent over backwards" to meet the concerns of service agencies. Instead of providing all services directly through EES, Jerald now contracts many to community agencies that already offer quality programs.

It is crucial in co-locating services that clear lines of authority and procedures for settling policy differences be established at the outset. The Family Services Center was initially managed as a "community collaborative": Four agencies worked together on site, but there were no clear lines of authority at the staffing level. Neither was there a structure in place to handle conflicting policies and procedures. Despite the presence of a part-time building supervisor, each agency's workers continued to operate within its own organizational culture and set of rules. In the office, they divided themselves into education, health, and social service teams, which underscored professional differences; the teams rarely interacted. The school superintendent and the county HRS department director realized it was necessary to appoint a full-time manager with the authority to supervise all on-site staff and coordinate with agency administrators on policy issues. Thus, Linda Cantrell, a school administrator with experience in both special education and exceptional student education, was hired with the title of principal to manage the Family Services Center. Her goal was to "have it work as a whole instead of a fragmented service delivery model even though staff located at the center are employed by different agencies."

Although all three programs initially faced turf issues, they succeeded in building their comprehensive services with cooperation from the community. The programs all operate in relatively small communities where key administrators have formed personal relationships and conduct business through informal, as well as formal, channels. In Brattleboro, community leaders from health and mental health agencies, educational institutions, special education services, and daycare associations share a history of working relationships; many serve on each others' advisory boards or sit on the same town committees. They have organized activities together over the years and have learned to trust each other. This trust lays the foundation for innovative community ventures, even when the new sits uneasily with the old. Similarly, in Gainesville, Cantrell describes agency administrators' role as "facilitators." Even if bureaucratic rules pose setbacks, these administrators choose to help, rather than hinder, the program. "I can't think of any difficult personalities," says Cantrell. "....Most of the time, with bureaucratic rules, you can find a way to bend them and get around them in a legal way.... I have always seen that there are ways to make things happen in spite of the rules."

Negotiating Equity

The infusion of resources to a lead agency for a collaborative endeavor can be problematic. It can create a perception of inequity if other agencies are expected to provide services without the benefit of financial support. Or it can trigger envy among agencies that lack the time, resources, or entrepreneurship to go after new funding sources for themselves. When it was formed to house several state and federal programs, EES was viewed as a threat by private and public agencies in Brattleboro. Although it was not taking money away from these agencies—there were no local competitors for its federal grants—there was ill-feeling, nevertheless; EES was being funded generously at a time when state money for human services was being cut. As a way to negotiate more equity, and avert any resentment, EES administrators have learned to share the program's resources with local agencies that serve children, thereby enhancing its image in the community. Funds are channelled to local providers and surplus funds are shared outside formal contracts. For example, when EES received private grant money for a summer camp that already had sufficient support, Jerald notified the local YMCA, youth serving agencies, and daycare centers that EES had scholarship money for children to attend these agencies' summer programs. "It's important if you're a program that's got some money to share it with agencies that are getting cut left and right," says Jerald.

Managing Co-location

A multiservice center with outposted staff members creates a novel work environment: The staff needs to be oriented to a common mission and organizational culture. Managers must work to build staff cohesion and alleviate sources of tension or awkwardness. They will be facilitated in these efforts if they maintain open channels of communication and good working relationships with the head agencies represented by co-located staff. When they are assigned to multiservice centers, staff from other agencies must adopt a holistic approach to family support and must be flexible in interpreting their job descriptions. The Family Services Center solved these problems during its initial phase of operations, but it was a challenge: Lines of authority had to be defined; different operating philosophies and procedures had to be worked out; and a team had to be assembled. One of the first issues Cantrell worked on was clarifying governance issues. When she joined the program, she found "that half of the people worked for me and half didn't." She had to carefully arrange with other agencies her authority as site supervisor, a difficult process.

Through many hours of negotiation, Cantrell worked out an agreement with other agency supervisors in which she participates in screening, interviewing, and selecting staff to be outposted to the Family Services Center. She supervises their work and takes part in evaluating their performance. While outposted staff accept Cantrell's supervision within the framework of the program, they also report to their agency for professional supervision. "The issue of who governs is really important in this kind of an enterprise. That has to be established and some agency has to take the lead," Cantrell says. "It just happens that the school board is the predominant supplier of people and money and has taken the lead, though we look at everybody as being very much on equal footing with us." Co-located staff are chosen carefully, not only for their competence in their field, but also for their willingness to "take on a whole concept of care" that transcends specialization. Buying into this common goal of serving families allows them to work together, despite the training and background differences among them.

Developing Respectful Partnerships

While it is efficient to have a lead agency coordinate a multiagency initiative, it is also important that all agencies have the opportunity to exercise leadership. Staff members at Early Education Services learned through their case-management meetings that they could not always be the ones to facilitate discussions and assume the lead role; the initiative of other agencies had to be respected as well. Similarly, Cantrell learned that "It's real important for somebody in a position such as mine not to try to take credit for everything. Let other people have their say, let other people win, let other people get the credit for things that they've been involved in."

Mutual respect for different perspectives is a key component of effective collaboration (Benard, 1989:75) and must be a guiding principle at family support centers. In negotiating for a psychologist for the Family Services Center, for example, Cantrell asked Mental Health Services to provide a part-time person. According to Jill Baird of Mental Health Services, Cantrell was "very open to asking us, 'Tell us about your service, and let me tell you about mine. What's it going to look like together?'" Agreeing on a definition of "mental health professional" took some time for the administrators of the two agencies and was "frustrating" because each had a different concept of what services were needed. Cantrell wanted a contracted staff person to serve any individual member of a participating family, while the administrators at Mental Health Services wanted to limit the service population to young children. The agency administrators explained to Cantrell that the psychologist to be outposted to the Family Services Center worked for their early childhood program, not their comprehensive outpatient program which serves youth. Since most of the Family Services Center's population would be young children, the demand for services would be great enough to fill the co-located staffer's case load. Older school children could be referred to Mental Health Services and accommodated in their other programs.

There was give and take throughout the negotiating process. Mental Health Services adopted new procedures for working with the Family Services Center: Administrators agreed to Cantrell's participation in interviewing candidates—the agency had not done this before—and to instituting a system of joint supervision. The process was "all mutual definition along the way," according to Baird and was an experience that benefited both parties. The Family Services Center acquired the psychologist it needed, and Mental Health Services expanded its repertoire from an in-home and in-school model to include services to center-based parent support groups. Moreover, the following year, the Family Services Center contracted with Mental Health Services to provide a second mental health counselor to work with children six to twelve years of age.

Lessons for Practitioners

In order to provide comprehensive, cost-effective, and integrated services, many family centers join forces with other social service agencies. Existing community resources can be leveraged to position a center to work with—instead of competing against—other service providers. Adherence to the following principles can facilitate a cooperative effort:

1. *Working with other agencies and sharing resources can extend the range of services of any one program.* There is no single method that works best for a program. Instead, it is wise to adopt multiple avenues of referrals, contract for services and other resources, and expand on initial service arrangements. The staff needs to commit a significant amount of time to networking with the staff at other agencies and learning about their programs.

2. *Procedures for working out conflict are necessary to sustain collaboration.* When agencies with different organizational cultures try to work together, conflict is bound to occur. Creating a collaborative effort requires a commitment to family support that allows decision makers to remove or work around restrictive rules. But, even the best laid plans cannot always preclude conflict over roles and responsibilities. Well defined systems of communication and conflict resolution procedures need to be established, if these differences are to be worked out.

3. *Respect is basic to collaboration.* Learning to listen and adopt the perspective of other agencies is a helpful strategy. Every agency has its own deeply embedded and specialized policies, procedures, and value systems. Perspective taking—putting oneself in the position of a small program with great flexibility or that of a large bureaucracy with its rigidly prescribed rules—can create a better understanding of each agency's strengths and challenges, as well as its potential contributions to the collaboration. Recognizing the expertise of other agencies and working from there will provide an opportunity to create new programs, develop alternatives to problematic situations, and encourage further collaboration to serve children and families. Even if a collaboration has a lead agency, everyone has to share in the labor and, ultimately, the success of a family support effort.

4. *Participants must be open to learning a new language of collaboration.* Collaboration is designed and implemented in a climate of uncertainty and ambiguity. Those involved in the experience—planners and staff—spend considerable time groping in the dark as they shape a new blueprint of action. Part of the process involves creating a mutual language of activities, staffing, schedules, and referrals. When agencies contract or co-locate staff, agreement on the definitions of positions such as "social worker," "psychologist," and "education specialist" require negotiations about roles and expectations.

5. *A collaboration works best when agencies both give and get.* Reciprocity can cover a wide range of activities: information delivery, training, services provision, and funding. Agency staffs need incentives to work together; self-interest can be an important motivating factor. When agencies fill gaps in each other's programs, they optimize a community's resources. They open new opportunities for service delivery and extend the support available, not only to each other, but, most importantly, to their mutual constituencies.

4 Designing Services for Young Children

It seems reasonable to assume that disadvantage results from a combination of adverse environmental features, and that the goal of children's services ought to be to improve the overall quality of children's environments in ways that make them more conducive to satisfying lives and healthy development.

Mary Jo Bane (1991:3)

All three programs in this study contain the components that the National Governors' Association identifies as necessary to any readiness program: early childhood education; primary health care; and parenting education. Yet, none of the three programs resembles the other: They offer services in different types of settings; they emphasize different service components; and the structures of the organizations themselves differ. This is the way it should be: If the programs looked alike, they would not be meeting the unique needs of their respective communities.

Any family support program must be designed for the convenience of the specific population it serves. While one mode of service delivery may work for the majority of participants, additional, more limited forms of delivery will probably be needed to ensure that everyone is reached. EES is primarily a home visiting program; yet it became clear that it needed to deliver other services through center-based community programs. Conversely, it became apparent that The Center and the Family Services Center needed to maintain a home visiting component in order to reach all eligible families.

Services to promote the well-being of children include not only those that directly engage the child, but also parent education programs that enhance parents' capacity to nurture their child's development. This chapter describes the ways our three programs deliver education and health services in a variety of places: in the home; at daycare and in preschool; and at the public school itself. Table 4 (p. 42) summarizes each program's services for children.

Contexts for Service Delivery

In the Home

Home visiting is used for service delivery in many family support programs, particularly those for families with children from birth to age three. The rationale for using home visits varies across programs, but what emerges, quite consistently, are the following assumptions or beliefs:

> That a child's primary and best teacher is his or her parent; that the home represents the child's—and the parent's—most familiar, hence most comfortable, environment; that the home may be more appropriate for reaching disenfranchised or otherwise hard-to-reach parents; that the home allows a parent and/or child to interact one-on-one with the visitor; that the home is a more likely setting in which to reach the parent rather than waiting for the parent to visit a center; and that the home visit may well be less expensive and more cost-effective than center-based treatment (Gamse and Weiss, 1987:10).

Individual goals need to be set for every family participating in a program, but the schedule for progressing through should not be set by rigid parenting curricula. EES home visitors have goals for what they want to accomplish during each visit, but they also have a philosophy: Be flexible. A home visitor may need to change her agenda if a parent has a specific issue to discuss or a child has something special to share (Windham County Family Support Program, 1992:3).

Engaging in a developmentally appropriate activity with the child and talking to the parent about child development are meant to be components of each home visit. But "it doesn't always work out that way," says the former director of Parents As Teachers in Brattleboro, "and it varies a lot from family to family and what the concerns are at a particular time." This variability comes from the home visitor's readiness to deal with other family problems—health, housing, or

Table 4 Services for Children in Each Program

Services for Children	Program: *Early Education Services*	*The Center*	*Family Services Center*
Daycare (provided or referred)	✓	✓	✓
Home visits	✓	✓	✓
Developmental activities for children under age 3	✓	✓	✓
Preschool (Ages 4–5)	✓	✓	✓
Health screenings	✓	✓	✓
Easing transition to kindergarten	✓	✓	✓
Parent-child activities	✓	✓	✓
Integrating handicapped children into program		✓	

unemployment. Home visits are personal events, catered to each family's situation: Critical family needs may require attention before the home visitor can turn to more general parenting issues. The former director of PAT describes the ideal home visit as one that includes children and parents in a holistic way:

> The parent and I are going to make a crib mobile for the baby, and, as we make it, we talk about what it does for the baby, that this movement is going to stimulate the child's vision as she tracks the movement in the crib, and hears the tinkling of the metal....The parent is making it [the mobile] and getting information about child development at the same time, and then working with the baby with the finished product....That would be a model that involved her in making it, learning about it, and actually carrying it out with the child.

Home visitors at EES find that parents new to the program generally agree with the home visitor's ideas about parenting styles. As they become more comfortable with the home visitor, however, they begin to open up and make decisions about what does and does not feel right. Taking control of the family situation is something that the EES staff encourages parents to do. Key to this process, as one home visitor puts it, is "letting them (the families) know that they have control....They have to want what we're doing."

Dot Marsden, the first director of Brattleboro's PAT program and now the early education specialist at EES reflects: "What I've learned over the years is that you can't teach somebody something that they don't want to know. So, it's very important to be able to talk to parents and find out what their concerns are, and then problem solve with them. Lots of times, we're concerned about things that they don't see as problems. And that's where the hitch comes in." On the whole, Marsden reports, most parents appreciate the advice they receive. An EES parent agrees: "Sometimes it's good to have an outside opinion—and from somebody who has been educated in childrearing—to let you know that you're doing the right thing."

Although The Center primarily provides on-site services, it has instituted a limited home visiting program. The Center does home visits for the area's Head Start families. These sixty families receive two home visits a year from a Head Start teacher and a parent liaison. The fall visit is made by the teacher, since the purpose is for the teacher and parent to develop an individual education plan (IEP) for the child. The teacher and the parent liaison make the spring visit together: The teacher reviews the IEP, and the liaison completes a file update on needed family services and makes the appropriate referrals. A guide to community resources is given to the parent at each visit.

Staff representatives of the Florida First Start program—the component of the Family Services Center that focuses on children from birth to age three—make home visits to screen children, referring those with developmental delays to specialists. Staff representatives also offer individualized parenting sessions. A family receives between four and nine visits a year, depending on need. Staff of the Family Services Center's Even Start program—for children from birth to age seven—make monthly home visits. The home visitors take materials from the toy and book lending library and offer them to parents on a check-out basis. They also give the parents "Start Thinking" boxes which contain activity packets that demonstrate how parents can use materials commonly found in the home to interact with their children in a developmentally constructive way. Anne Young, the early childhood specialist, says, "When you first make a home visit with a two year old, you don't know where he's functioning. We start with activities at a basic developmental level, let's say six months, and move upward until we find an appropriate activity. We leave the activity packet with the parent and we might include something that will push the child toward the next level."

Home Daycare

One way to improve the well-being of many children in a community is to help home daycare providers improve the quality of their care. Through its Comprehensive Child Development Program (CCDP) grant, EES can include in its training those home care providers whose groups include children from families enrolled in the CCDP program. Additionally, these providers can attend training at EES and take education and early childhood development classes at the community college, with their tuition fees paid for by CCDP. Janet Gross, a former coordinator of children's programs at EES, instituted visits to each home daycare provider once a month for a training session. Gross (1991:4) finds that "family daycare providers most need a sounding board, a non-threatening model, and an extra hand. They need concrete information for specific problems. They need to see what children can be like when cared for appropriately."

The Family Services Center participated in a Family Daycare Homes Enhancement Program, funded in Alachua County in 1991 and 1992. The goals of this program were to help daycare providers develop comprehensive early learning programs, especially for language development, and to establish a link between the providers and the school system.

Although home daycare providers operate in direct competition with her programs, Center director Kathy Brendza actively supports them. She sees this support as a way to improve the quality of daycare for Leadville children who are not enrolled in Center programs. When The Center takes in children from home daycare when a provider is ill, the reliability of home daycare increases.

Center-based Services

Programs serving children four and older are primarily center-based. Steps that need to be taken to establish such a program include: choosing a curriculum, determining how to mix into classes children enrolled under different federal and state programs, and developing parent involvement activities. The Center was committed to designing a child-centered curriculum. Says Superintendent McCabe, "If you're running an adult-centered kindergarten, then kids who are not developmentally ready (for school) don't do very well. But if you're running a child-centered kindergarten, it's okay....You're going to meet their needs anyway."

Brendza, the program director, designed The Center's preschool to cater to the specific needs of Leadville's four- and five-year-old children. She chose the child-focused High/Scope curriculum because, "We looked around at a couple of different curricula, and it best fit what we wanted to do. We wanted children to learn about solving problems. We wanted them to learn about making choices, because we knew that children on drugs obviously don't know about making correct choices. Somewhere along the line they've not been able to weigh out the good and the bad. Or girls become pregnant. We feel it's a choice rather than an accident, that they've not had a problem-solving component in their life earlier...." With High/Scope, the child directs his or her own interests and activities, in contrast to curricula that call for teachers to lead all classroom activities while children listen passively. Some Leadville parents, used to traditional education, have requested a more academic preschool with flash cards and phonics. But, Brendza stands by High/Scope, judging it a better way for children to learn.

Unlike traditional Head Start programs, Brendza mixes Head Start and non-Head Start preschoolers in one class. "The Head Start people asked us, 'How can you do that?'" she recounts. "'Head Start children need different education totally than your other children.' And we said, 'Tell us why you think that is. Tell us what the different education component is.' 'Well,' they answered, 'they (the Head Start children) need a language base, they need hands on. They need teacher-pupil exchanges, they need all this creative preschool.' Well, what child doesn't need that? They all need that." Superintendent McCabe adds, "Plus, you get the best vocabulary development by putting them (Head Start children) with kids with stronger language skills." This was also the rationale for The Center to move handicapped children from a special program run by a nonprofit organization in an isolated facility and mainstream them into Center classes. Parents of all the children are satisfied with this situation.

Involving parents in their children's education is the most challenging task Kathy Brendza faces at The Center. Because of the parents' diverse schedules, The Center has had to develop innovative ways to link parents with their children's learning activities. Parents are invited to monthly dinners where, for one dollar a person, they can eat in the cafeteria with their children and talk informally with the teachers. The Center also videotapes classes so parents can observe their children's activities. Field trips are a particular draw; The Center never has trouble finding enough parents to accompany the children to the Denver zoo and other attractions.

The Family Services Center's early childhood program is a key component in meeting its goal to "improve the quality of early childhood experiences for all children in the community." The staff in the infant-toddler room engage the children in a play-based curriculum with a strong language development component and check them for developmental milestones. Similarly, activities in the preschool room for children ages two-and-a-half to three are also play-based and characterized by "a whole language approach." Weekly parent-child activities complement the child-centered curriculum. This curriculum has been put together using a variety of resources, including materials developed by the National Center for Family Literacy, High/Scope, and Family Reading programs. Among the staff's goals for these programs are developing a child's self-esteem and providing a "solid beginning" so children can take full advantage of their schooling.

The children's programs of the Family Services Center are part of a collaborative effort that "moves in concentric circles outward" to other Gainesville programs. In an effort to strengthen the link between school sponsored programs, two staff members from the Head Start Prekindergarten program, established in elementary schools, have been assigned to enroll preschool children through the Family Services Center. Families already involved in the district's preschool programs are often referred to the Family Services Center for support services.

Programs to ready children for school often provide assistance in easing the transition to kindergarten. Typically, they share their records with the elementary schools and arrange to have their teachers meet with the kindergarten teachers to discuss the children's needs and strengths. The Center's transition activities cater to special needs children and are restricted to a meeting of the children's parents with teachers and other relevant staff from both schools. One parent of a special needs child reports, "When my son was about to enter kindergarten, nine educators came to a meeting for a whole hour, just about him. The principal of the elementary school, the school speech therapist, the school counselor, Kathy Brendza, his preschool teacher, my husband and myself, and others."

While teachers and administrators from the elementary school would like to extend this transition process to include all incoming children, The Center has reservations. As one Center administrator put it, opening the records of Center children to kindergarten teachers could result in "predetermining what the children are supposed to be."

EES also facilitates children's transition from its preschool to the public kindergartens. The preschool teachers meet with the kindergarten teachers to discuss the capabilities of the children and to give the teachers files that include the children's test results and an inventory of their strengths and weaknesses. The teachers continue to communicate after the children enter kindergarten. "The schools acknowledge," says a former EES administrator, "that our evaluation of a child's strengths and weaknesses is more valid than what they can do in a single half day with hundreds of other kids passing through the preschool screening." Confidentiality can be an issue, however. After one school principal voiced concern about this factor, it was arranged for parents to sign releases before the EES preschool teachers could share information about the children with the elementary school.

In the Public Schools

The staff of early childhood family support programs (even those that are connected to the school district) are concerned about the schools that their children will eventually enter. Elementary schools usually lag behind early education programs in developing child-centered curricula and support services for the family. This difference is not surprising. Early education programs typically have greater freedom to implement innovative programs than do public schools, anchored in long-standing practices. In Leadville, even with a superintendent and an elementary school principal both committed to change (the principal eliminated kindergarten screening, cut down on the use of workbooks, and began introducing children to "writing" at very early ages), it takes years to alter traditional practices. Often, the "most experienced" teachers are people who have taught for decades and may be very set in their ways of teaching. Leadville kindergarten teachers report having trouble with children coming from The Center: The creativity promoted in Center preschool programs does not fit well in the traditional (more passive, teacher controlled) kindergarten classroom.

The Center's success in mainstreaming handicapped children has influenced the practice of the town's only elementary school. Leadville's elementary school principal Larry Marriott has reformed elementary school special education in his school. Testing for "handicapping conditions" is now done only at a parent's request, and teachers are instructed to address the needs of children of all abilities in their classrooms. It is anticipated that these practices will be adopted to some extent by other school districts surrounding Lake County.

The sources of EES' greatest influence on moving the family support philosophy into the elementary schools is its federal Follow Through grant for selected K–3 classrooms. Follow Through funds provide the following resources: paraprofessionals to increase the amount of attention given to each child; special parenting meetings and child care and transportation for those who attend them; and the services of an EES staff person to act as liaison between the school and the Follow Through parents, to encourage parents to visit the school and volunteer in the classroom.

Family liaisons and preschool teachers from the three programs often find themselves acting as de facto advocates for parents of children in the school district. Having gained the trust of parents, the family liaisons or preschool teachers receive calls from them—often years after their children have left the preschool or family support program—asking for their help in dealing with a problem in the elementary school. The parent may need moral support during a parent-teacher conference, for example, or help in asking the school to review the way it is handling a child's behavior or academic problem. In Leadville, the family advocates provide such assistance. McCabe states, "If there's an argument between the school district and the parent, they have to side with the parents. They can't side with the district. They have to serve the parent and be an advocate for the parent."

The Family Services Center staff helps parents of school age children by reviewing report cards and coaching them on effective communication for parent-teacher conferences. This kind of support, says a Family Services Center staff member, "means a lot to parents, and it helps them get out there and do what they should be doing for their children." Parents at the Family Services Center participate enthusiastically in group discussions on parenting topics that include discipline, "quality time," and reading regularly to children. One Gainesville mother illustrates the impact that Family Services Center programs have had on her home environment. Her six-year-old daughter began to excel in school, she says, "because they [the Family Services Center workers] helped me cope with [her] more....Before I lay around when she came home with her homework....I learned how serious it was for parents to really get up when a kid brings a paper in, you know, look at it and make sure you help them if they need help and all, and say something nice if they do something nice."

Through innovative use of the Chapter 1 program, which funds about half of its adult computer lab, the Family Services Center also weaves together adult education programs and student classroom activities. Teachers in the adult education program have worked with school teachers on developing joint assignments for parents and children. The adult education teachers go through the assignments first with parents, enabling the parents, in turn, to help their children with their homework. Giving their children this kind of support empowers parents, reinforces their children's positive view of them, increases their understanding of what their children learn in school, and fosters closer home-school ties.

Because their parent involvement activities have been successful, the staff of the Family Services Center is beginning to train family advocates who work in different elementary schools within the district on outreach strategies to parents and ways to encourage positive school-home partnerships.

Key Components of Early Childhood Education

- Developmentally appropriate activities and curricula for children birth to age five
- Quality care for children
- Parent involvement in children's education
- Transition activities from preschool to kindergarten
- Provision of health services

Providing Health Services

All three programs are struggling to piece together health services they can provide on site or through referrals to other agencies, in an effort to fill the service gaps that have been created by the national health care crisis. A report issued by the Center for the Future of Children (1992:8) makes the point: "Because health plays such a pivotal role in the development and well-being of children, we believe that children and pregnant women cannot afford to wait while the health care crisis deepens to the point where reforms are unavoidable." The three programs in this study—each of which attends to the health and nutrition of pregnant women and children—are excellent examples of responses to this crisis.

Of the three programs, the Family Services Center, with the co-location of a nurse practitioner on site, provides the most direct health care to its families. Open to all children and adults in the community who are Medicaid eligible, its clinic provides preventive health care (including immunizations) in a more personal way, and with less waiting time, than the local public health clinic. The clinic also provides screening services for children in the Head Start and preschool programs of neighborhood elementary schools. As a complement to these services, health and nutrition education is incorporated into the preschool curriculum and in parent education meetings.

In July 1993, after negotiations between the school district and the local public health department, the latter assumed management of the Family Services Center clinic. Ann Crowell (who succeeded Cantrell as director) considers this a positive step in strengthening the quality of the program's health services. A public health officer will establish and monitor regular office procedures and will supervise the nursing staff and interns from the University of Florida's College of Nursing. The new arrangement will extend the hours of the clinic to full time. It will also facilitate communication between agencies and families regarding changes in state Medicaid regulations.

An on-site health clinic, whose staff works closely with that of the family support center that houses it, can achieve remarkable improvements in the overall health of families that have been mistreated for years by the conventional medical, educational, and social systems. One little boy in Gainesville who had serious behavior problems serves as a case in point. The school had dealt with him through repeated suspensions and, finally, reassignment to a school for "special" children, where he was locked in solitary confinement for four hours a day. Medical practitioners said his health was fine and went no further. It was not until a family liaison worker and the clinic nurse from the Family Services Center became involved that the child was determined to need Ritalin medication. Since the time he started taking the medication, his behavior has improved so dramatically that he has been awarded model citizen citations by his school. The child's mother says:

> ...and from the medicine that they gave to him down here, it was like turning darkness into light for me. I mean, I came back and I told her (a Family Services Center staff member), "I don't know how to thank you. If I had a whole lot of money, I would buy you anything in the world right now that you want because you gave me my son back." Because the system did not give him to me. I asked for him back, but they didn't do it.

At EES, all families enrolled in the CCDP-funded Windham County Family Support Program receive dental and health services from private providers under Medicaid. Under an agreement with the Vermont Health Department, the program provides health services to pregnant women through the Medicaid Outreach Program, which gives priority to pregnant women under 21 years of age. The CCDP health coordinator (a nurse) screens families for health care needs and provides preventive health care education during home visits. EES also actively refers families to established programs. Children are screened at the private, nonprofit Prouty Center, which educates developmentally delayed children. Pregnant women and mothers of young children are referred to the WIC program to obtain supplemental food.

The Center links families to Leadville health practitioners in several ways. First, it maintains close contact with the local health department, whose characteristically quick response is an excellent example of the benefits of good collaboration. The Center routinely goes through its records to check children's immunization status. Coordination regarding immunization schedules has increased since the time Center staff called dozens of families to say that if their children did not get their shots immediately, they would not be allowed back to school. Almost 80 people showed up at the public health clinic the next day! Second, The Center transports children to doctors and dentists when their parents are not available to do so. Third, The Center encourages proper nutrition among its families. Hot, healthy meals are served to children on site, and The Center is a sponsor of the Share Colorado program. This state-wide endeavor provides people with food at low-cost in exchange for community service.

Lessons for Practitioners

Achieving the maximum benefits for children requires that programs respond to families' expressed needs, as well as to the larger needs of the community. Responsiveness, flexibility, concern, and vision are all attributes of an effective program. Those who are charged with establishing or modifying education and health services as part of a family support program must set the program up to do the following:

1. *Concentrate services where they are most responsive to families' needs.* Most programs will have one dominant means of service delivery. They may, additionally, need to offer alternative and more limited means of delivery, for example, a small home visiting program to supplement center-based services. Find out what families want and need.

2. *Teach parents the skills they need to parent well, and teach those skills in a setting and manner that empowers the participants.* Especially important are opportunities for parents to teach each other, exchange ideas, and form support networks.

3. *Encourage staff to give families as much control over their lives as they can handle.* A delicate balancing act is required in guiding parents where necessary, while directing explicit behavior change only in areas where such change is crucial. Promote independence step by step.

4. *Create exciting, innovative early education programs.* Parents may not understand the goals of the new developmentally appropriate curricula and child-centered classrooms as well as the importance of

play in learning and development. The benefits of such a program must be explained to them. Invite them into the classroom to observe and to learn how different activities and materials help develop their children's skills.

5. *Discuss and model the different ways parents need to be involved in their children's lives.* Develop innovative programs to encourage this behavior. Have parents new to the program talk with parents who have seen improvement in their children's lives because of such involvement.

6. *Develop clear, practical exercises that facilitate teacher-parent interaction.* Provide parents with all the support they need in dealing with the schools, but do not forget also to encourage the schools to become more family friendly.

7. *Be as flexible as possible with grant and program criteria.* The Center's success in combining Head Start students with other preschoolers proves that the way a program is normally implemented may not make sense for every community. Be as creative with the guidelines as possible.

5 Designing Services for Parents

To be successful, policies and programs cannot concentrate solely on the child but must simultaneously address the needs of two generations—the parent and the child—for they are interdependent.... A proper role of the school is the development of both the family and the child.

Council of Chief State School Officers (1989:6)

What does it mean to offer comprehensive family support? What does a two-generation approach entail? The complexity of family-focused intervention is illustrated in the following case, described by a staff person at a family support center:

> The court had taken her children. We knew from the first moment that she had a lot to offer but she was trying to satisfy a court performance. She was a very shapely girl and had on clothes that were so tight you wouldn't know how she got in them; they were so short. She had a ring in her nose; she had her hair dyed different colors. I had to tell her what she looked like....And I said, "If I was the judge, I probably would rule the same way because of how you look and dress and act." So I said, "You are a mother and you are going to look and act like a parent."
>
> One day I went out in the hallway and there stood a beautiful young lady who had dyed her hair one color, had taken the ring out

> of her nose, and had on a dress that was appropriate. I had to hug her. Her therapist later said, "I want to tell you something that will make your day. D. said that she appreciates you so much; you talk to her like a mother and she never had that before."
>
> We (staff) tried to help her meet some of the requirements that she had gotten from the court in order to try to get her children back. We did get her in school, took her down to a mental health agency to check that she was free of drugs. We did get her a job. She has a home now and one of the kids. She's working on getting the other one back.

When parents are supported by a program both as individuals and as family, they are more likely to fulfill their parental roles effectively. Such support, along with the provision of related services, conveys the message that adults can change; it also nurtures their potential for development (Weissbourd and Kagan, 1989:22). As our case example illustrates, comprehensive family support begins with a staff that recognizes and builds on parent strengths. It requires the coordination of many services—mental health, parenting skills, adult education, housing, and a job—to meet a parent's needs. It means helping a parent navigate through various public systems: She may need help, for example, in enrolling in a WIC supplementary food program or in registering for, and then completing, an associate's degree program at the local community college. Providing this kind of assistance takes many hours of staff time. The range of services parents receive in the three programs is summarized in Table 5.

It is not enough, however, just to *provide* services to parents. The *way* services are delivered to parents is equally important. Staff must:

- Recognize and build on parent strengths
- Employ a nonjudgmental, caring, and respectful approach
- Provide honest feedback
- Empower parents in their decisionmaking
- Show high expectation and faith in parents' ability to succeed
- Provide a role model of a hard working, caring, and dedicated community member
- Encourage parents to provide informal support for each other, within and outside the program
- Offer ongoing assessment and feedback on a parent's goals

Providing Supportive Services

The three programs in this study are noteworthy for the kind of personal and individual attention they give families. Each identifies

Table 5 **Types of Services Parents Receive Through the Three Programs**

Services	**Program** *Early Education Services*	*The Center*	*Family Services Center*
Parent involvement activities	✓	✓	✓
Parenting classes	✓	✓	✓
Parent support groups	✓		✓
Individual counseling on personal or family problems	✓	✓	✓
Adult education	✓	✓	✓
Vocational training	✓		✓
English as a Second Language classes		✓	
Referrals for legal, housing, employment, and other social service assistance	✓	✓	✓
Health counseling and services	✓		✓
Financial services (loan programs, direct AFDC assistance)	✓		✓
Coordination and referrals to substance abuse programs	✓		✓

individual family needs through in-take interviews. At the Family Services Center, the initial needs assessment is the basis for a family plan drawn up by the parents and a staff member, usually the family liaison specialist. Parents tell the staff member what it is they want to do, and the staff helps them outline a plan to meet their goals. The staff works with the parents to identify priorities and to resolve their most pressing needs which are typically in the areas of housing, economic assistance, health, domestic violence, divorce, suicide risk, and child abuse and neglect.

The staff of each program employs a nonjudgmental and respectful approach. At EES, the objective in conducting needs assessments is not to determine a family's weaknesses, but rather to identify its strengths, resources, and existing support systems. Periodic assessment continues throughout the family's time in the program. Staff members respect participants' decisions and attempt to interpret family concerns as objectively as possible. They accept parents where they are emotionally and then guide them in their personal development. As Jerald says, "We try to distinguish what we want and what they (participants) want and make sure that we're not saying that something we want is what they want necessarily. A parent may want to join a Weight Watchers class. Then that's what we help them do, even though what we think they need is to stop smoking. We start with them."

There are times, however, when a staff person has to be firm, and to convince a parent that for the good of the child and family, certain behavioral changes are required. As our opening story illustrates, a mix of respect for, and shaping of, parent decisions is important. There are no easy solutions to manage complex personal and family problems; staff must deal with the issues on a case-by-case basis.

The programs, either through staff work on site or through referrals to mental health services in the community, provide a range of support and counseling for families. Some families simply need a sympathetic ear. "You have to be able to listen to parents," says Family Services Center's Phyllis McKnight, a family liaison worker. "Many of these parents have never really had anyone who they feel cares enough to listen to them. I'm not a counselor by profession, but I end up having to do a lot of listening. It's not like they're seeking you to solve [problems]. They just want you to hear what's going on."

Families who need more than a willing ear are connected to appropriate agencies. The Center in Leadville, for example, contracts with West Mental Health Center, a private agency, to provide services to Head Start families. Family counseling is often needed. Many parents in Leadville are under a lot of stress, as they try to combine jobs and childrearing. "Parents are trying to do several different jobs in a very limited amount of time," says Theresa Wallace, West Mental Health Center's director. "When parents come home, they're tired and their children need help with homework or reading. But there's dinner and baths....Many of them work in jobs that don't have benefits like sick pay. To stay home with a sick child means to miss a day's pay....And kids worry about their parents driving over the mountain passes. Believe it or not, I have kids who worry if mom or dad is a little late."

IMPROVING PARENTS' EDUCATION

Parent participation in a child's education is enhanced when parents, themselves, have an adequate education. There are various ways to encourage parents to continue their education. The strategies used by the programs in this study to provide adult education are listed below.

Early Education Services

- Refers parents to state adult education program
- Offers home tutoring
- Counsels teen parents to remain in high school
- Helps parents enroll in community college

The Center

- Houses adult education program of community college

Family Services Center

- Offers on-site adult education
- Helps parents enroll in community college

Parents who seek to improve their education through family support programs enjoy advantages they are unlikely to receive from regular adult education programs. Particularly important for parents whom the staff defines as "fragile"—teenage parents, parents under stress, parents who fear going back to school, and those who have low self-esteem—is the staff's intensive and ongoing support. Access to a reassuring staff in a friendly environment helps parents take the first steps, as well as remain on track in meeting their education goals. Programs are flexible. If parents miss adult education classes at the Family Services Center, for example, they can continue where they left off when they return. The most critical staff function is to actively encourage participants in their uphill struggle to get a GED. The high quality of the staff also provides parents with role models of hard working, caring, and dedicated people.

What is noteworthy about the adult education components of the family support programs is that they offer more than academic preparation; students are treated with respect and learn to make choices about how to pursue their education. Parents in the family literacy program of EES can enroll in the state of Vermont's home-based adult basic education program, or they can choose to design another education plan. "I think the thing that pushes them [parents] away a lot of times is feeling that they're going to need to work on some kind of adult education skills," says Diane Coleman, who ran the Even Start family literacy program for EES. "I think that's very threatening to folks who haven't finished high school." Consequently, at EES, the adult component is designed to "keep things as flexible as you can." Parents write and talk to their home visitors about what it is they want to work on, whether reading to their children or developing their own writing skills.

Similarly, Bebe Fearnside, the supervisor of all school-based early childhood programs in the Alachua county district, says the approach to adult education is "not just getting your GED with pencil and paper, but getting it with some kind of dignity." Recruitment for the adult education classes of the Family Services Center initially involved a door-to-door campaign to ask parents if they would be interested in learning computer skills. Aware of the stigma associated with enrolling in a GED program, the staff decided not to mention GEDs at this point. "People think the reason you're getting the GED is because you couldn't get through high school," adds Fearnside. By contrast, enrolling in a computer course gives people the sense that they are participating in something more important, and more advanced, a step that can give them the confidence to pursue a GED course as well. And for those who in the end do not complete the GED, additional vocational training is available.

The staff of a program must stay alert to needs that participants have which, if unattended, limit their success in a work environment. The staff at the Family Services Center, for example, observed that mothers who have led isolated lives typically lack the social skills to function effectively in a group setting. To address this problem, a life skills component was added to the curriculum of the adult computer lab.

Parents are motivated to learn when staff have high expectations for them and faith in their ability to succeed. Teen parents in EES programs say that the home visitors open new horizons for them, encouraging them to remain in school and inspiring some of them to go on to college. In Gainesville, parents spoke of how the Family Services Center's staff challenges and encourages them, and demonstrates continued interest in them even after they obtain their GED. One parent sums it up: "They teach you not to stay where you are. They help teach you to come up. You can get your GED. You can go to Santa Fe (the local community college). They just push you, because they can see the potential in you and, therefore, they will push you to your limits."

Staff members need to realize, however, that their support does not guarantee a participant's success. Phyllis McKnight, a family liaison worker at the Family Services Center, conducts a weekly follow up of parents who have been absent from education classes to encourage them in their school work. While her efforts sustain many parents for at least some period of time, one-third of parents do eventually drop out of the program. McKnight attributes student attrition to the need to take care of sick children, family transience, and stress from relationships and financial situations.

Improving Parents' Economic Situations

Helping families attain economic self-sufficiency is one of the long-term goals of family support programs. Since employers paying decent wages tend to require more than a high school diploma, all three programs in our study link parents to higher education through local community colleges. Parents are also counseled by the staff about the realities of the community's economic situation and the need to train for jobs for which there is and will be high demand. EES social worker Ann Darling explains to families that losing a job during a recession is not necessarily their fault. But, she stresses, they have control over what they can do to re-enter the market. She tells those who have been laid off from their jobs: "The kind of job you're qualified to get at this point, there are going to be very few of them any more." She then encourages them to make career shifts. "This is really a good time for you to get some training," she tells them. "We [EES] can help pay for that. We can help pay for child care while you're in training." Similarly, the staff at the Family Services Center tries to steer parents toward jobs in the health field, since four large hospitals are located in Gainesville.

Of the three programs, only the Family Services Center is directly linked with a welfare-to-work program, which, in Florida, is called "Project Independence." Mothers in Project Independence attend adult education and parenting classes, participate in parent-child activities, and get work-related experience by practicing clerical skills as support staff at the Family Services Center.

While trying to augment parents' earning capacity over the long run, family support programs also have to address the immediate needs of a population that is chronically short of money. At the Family Services Center, economic assistance is provided on site through a Department of Health and Rehabilitative Services employee who processes eligibility for food stamps, supplemental food assistance for pregnant and postpartum women and their infants and children (WIC), and cash payments to needy children and their parents. The Comprehensive Child Development Program (CCDP)-funded family support program of EES and the First Vermont Bank have created a Loan Fund Program for families who would not ordinarily qualify for a bank loan. The family support program has opened a savings account of $20,000 in the bank; the money is used as collateral for low interest (two percent) loans to its participating families. Monthly payments for loans are kept under $50 and no loan exceeds $1500. An important component of the loan fund is financial counseling for participants on topics that include money management and loan applications. Participants have taken out loans to purchase such items as cars and clothes dryers, to make home improvements, and to consolidate bills. The loan program has provided some families with their first experience in dealing with a lending institution and opening a savings account.

There is preliminary evidence that families enrolled in the CCDP program have benefitted economically as intended. First, more individual participants have jobs now than before they entered the program. Second, the average earned family income has doubled over a two-and-a-half year period from $9,000 to $18,000 (Windham County Family Support Program Data Report, April 1993).

EMPOWERING FAMILIES

> Empowerment is an intentional, ongoing process centered in the local community, involving mutual respect, critical reflection, caring, and group participation, through which people lacking an equal share of valued resources gain greater access to and control over those resources (Barr and Cochran, 1992:2).

Empowering families begins with a caring attitude on the part of a program's staff. This engenders a relationship of trust and moves parents to take control of their lives, and those of their children. One staff member from the Family Services Center explains: "We start out by letting them [parents] know that, even though this is an educationally-based program, we care more about the family than most school systems care. It's not just the child we're concentrating on. We care that you may face eviction. We care that your lights were turned off. Let us try to help you." This broad-based concern encourages parents to express their needs and aspirations, and to see that there are ways to resolve their problems. It is not a smooth process, and staff members have to remind themselves that a little change is good and not to expect too much, too fast.

Family support program staffs are painfully aware that many of their families have been promised much before and have been let down—by agencies, friends, and family members. A staff person says families are up against "generations of mistrust, helplessness, and hopelessness." Yet, the fact that most families remain in the programs and that it is easy to recruit new ones indicates that these initiatives do break down barriers and can help parents acquire self-esteem, strengthen parenting skills, and work toward self-sufficiency.

Participants in family support programs not only learn the academic skills that will help them become self-sufficient, they also become part of a social environment that boosts their confidence, gives them hope, and teaches them how to be in control of their lives. By focusing on the positive, the staff of family support programs helps families recognize the resources they have to deal with difficult situations. Program participants also learn from each other and offer encouragement in accomplishing their parenting or educational goals. One mother says, "We've formed one big family. I think the ladies share a lot of different things. We've bonded a close relationship being together for a good part of the day. So we look out for each other." Mothers of school-aged children who come for adult education classes join mothers of children in the early childhood program and hug and play with each other's children. As another puts it, "You just feel like you're a part of each other."

The staff members of family support programs prepare parents to deal with existing educational, health, and social service systems. At EES, they "model" for parents the experience of interacting with a public agency, showing them how to communicate their situation, ask questions, and negotiate services. The staff from all three programs sends families to other agencies for certain types of help so they can learn to seek assistance from more than one source, and to identify and negotiate access to a range of community resources—key steps to empowerment (Barr and Cochran, 1992:3). Parents also participate in an ongoing process of defining and reflecting upon their goals. At EES' Even Start program, each participant's education plan is updated every few months through a formal interview. This practice gives the parent an opportunity to identify, reassess, and work on goals. "What we have built into this system is a capacity to change direction, if parents decide that they would prefer to do something differently," says Diane Coleman, former director of EES' Even Start. "It's fine with us and it works for families."

Families are not forgotten after they are "weaned" from the programs. Occasional program support reinforces their sense of belonging. As one parent describes it, "They (staff members) don't give up on you once you get your diploma. They're still calling and finding whether there's a better job than what I have. It's not like you graduate now and it ends. I mean, they keep up with you." That is what gives adult education programs their special nature when they operate in the context of family support programs: Parents are not merely students; they are family.

Lessons for Practitioners

Family support is a total phenomenon: It embraces the needs of children, as well as parents, and it spans health, employment, education, and housing issues. While other programs in a community may provide similar services, family support programs stand apart in *how* they perform their services. The operation of the three programs in our study demonstrates the value of the following practices in working with families:

1. *Developing caring and respectful partnerships.* Parents are attracted to a program when they are treated with genuine concern and respect. They are then likely to *stay* in the program if they receive unconditional emotional support and are treated as responsible people. The relationship between program staff and participants is a mutual one in which each can learn from the other. They negotiate the terms of support that a staff member can give and the assistance a parent can expect.

2. *Being flexible.* Each family is unique. While a family support program offers a set of core services, goals are tailored, through needs assessments, to individual family situations. Some flexibility may be built into the structure of services, such as adult education and counseling services. In addition, the staff must be ready to modify a family's program to accommodate parent preferences or changing family circumstances. In every case, the program adheres to the principle of "families first."

3. *Setting high expectations.* As important as it is to create a caring environment for a family support program, so, too, is it important to create an environment of challenge and hope. Participants will be motivated to work toward their goals if the staff has high expectations and conveys confidence in their abilities. Carefully planned activities that confirm participants' progress will also foster their self-esteem and commitment to the program.

4. *Encouraging proactive participation.* Unlike the traditional human services paradigm that labels families as clients, family support programs view them as participants. Parents are active partners in identifying, modifying, and accomplishing their goals. All three programs engage parents in activities that strengthen parenting skills, increase family self-sufficiency, provide them with access to community services, and engender in them a sense of responsibility for other families in the community.

6 Staffing Programs with Caring and Creative People

We envision a system where early childhood and family support providers feel that parents and the general public value their work. We encourage talented people to enter the field, often to serve the communities in which they live. However, a career path that provides financial support for appropriate training, and compensation for increased competence and responsibilities is essential. Through financial and regulatory incentives, as well as public awareness, we can attract and retain the most caring and creative people in the country.

National Task Force on School Readiness (1991:31)

Not surprisingly, the staff of each of the three programs in our study is outstanding: It takes exemplary staff to make a model program. Since these programs are intended to help people in very vulnerable and personal parts of their lives—parenting, health, and education—the staff that works with the families must combine humanism with professionalism. Staffing decisions may well be the most critical decisions made by family support center program directors. In all three case studies, the directors have found ways to hire and retain excellent staff, in spite of financial and geographic constraints. Staff enthusiasm for the work is unmistakable.

- One EES home visitor says that if a parent calls her at home at night, she does not think of it as "work" infringing on her personal time; instead, she views it as a call from a friend.
- Women attending the Family Services Center's adult education program found a way to express gratitude toward their teacher

who stays late, comes in on her day off, and does not stop for lunch: They decided to take turns bringing her lunch everyday.

- A parent at The Center notices that "It doesn't matter if it's not your child's teacher. You walk down the hall and everybody says 'hi' to you. All the teachers care so much."

This chapter discusses the ways Early Education Services, The Center, and the Family Services Center attract and retain their excellent staffs. The directors of each program look for employees with personalities suited to the demands of the work. They then provide a supportive workplace with the following features: flexible schedules, staff development opportunities, and a management style that is open and consultative.

Hiring the Right Staff

The three programs vary in their staffing patterns. In keeping with its focus on daycare and preschool activities, The Center's staff consists mainly of child care providers and early childhood teachers. Staff members from other community agencies come to The Center to deliver health services, adult education, and parenting classes.

Both EES and The Family Services Center, in contrast, have a diverse staffing pattern consisting of home visitors, family liaison workers, social workers, nurses, and early childhood teachers. Key staff positions and their responsibilities are described in Table 6.

All three directors look for the best combination of personality, experience, and training to fill a staff position.

"If they are caring and nurturing, have empathy toward children, and have had some experience, then we know they're a candidate," says Brendza, director of The Center in Leadville.

Cantrell, of the Family Services Center, looks for staff members who believe that people in difficult situations have the potential to change their lives.

Jerald of EES reports, "I didn't want to hire people who had been doing classical case work for three years. I wanted people who would come in and sit on the floor and play with a baby...."

One advantage in starting up new programs is that the directors have the freedom to hire the staff of their choice. Brendza is reluctant to hire teachers with many years of traditional teaching, afraid that they would find it difficult to teach the child-directed High/Scope curriculum. Jerald and Cantrell feel that many applicants with master's of social work degrees are not "hands on enough" and are too rigid to be home visitors or family liaison specialists.

Table 6 Roles and Responsibilities of Key Staff Positions

Staff Positions	Description of Duties
Home Visitors / Parent Educators	Help parents find health care, daycare, adult education classes, housing, employment, or other needed services
	Engage in developmentally appropriate activities with the children
	Teach parenting skills
	Encourage parents to identify and meet their goals
Preschool Teachers	Prepare children for school through developmentally appropriate play and a child-based learning philosophy
	Screen children for possible cognitive delays
Early Childhood Specialists	Train and supervise home visitors; develop early childhood curriculum
Family Liaisons / Social Workers	Advocate for families who need services from other agencies
	Offer parenting classes and/or parent support groups
	Mediate conflicts and maintain open communication between program families and outside agencies
Adult Education Teachers	Offer GED, computer literacy, and other classes; help parents register for classes at local colleges
	Prepare parents to enter local job market
Nurse Practitioners	Offer on-site basic health care, including immunizations, health care information, and counseling
	Refer families to other clinicians or facilities
Program Directors	Oversee entire program, including collaborative partnerships, budget, funding, staff, and training

Staffing Issues

- Finding the right combination of personality, experience, and training to fill a position
- Hiring paraprofessionals from the community who can serve as role models for program participants
- Helping staff grow into new positions
- Providing on-going training for staff
- Preventing burnout
- Providing a flexible and supportive work environment
- Discouraging family over-dependence on staff
- Maintaining open and honest communication between staff and program directors

Paraprofessionals (usually parent educators, sometimes preschool teachers) are commonly hired on the basis of their personal qualities, rather than their credentials. Although they may have earned college degrees, they usually lack the specific departmental degrees or accreditations that would classify them as teaching professionals. Paraprofessionals are an invaluable resource for family support programs on several counts. They are more available than are professionals in the remote geographic areas in which programs often operate, and they can be paid more affordable wages. But, more important, paraprofessionals are often from the same socioeconomic circumstances as the program participants. Their first-hand knowledge of the issues confronting members of that community makes it easier for them to establish a rapport with program participants than it would be for outside professionals, a particular advantage for home visitors and family liaisons. Further, they can serve as valuable role models for participants: They demonstrate that high levels of responsibility can be assumed and substantial care given by someone who comes from the same background as they do.

The programs' openness to hiring on the strengths of an applicant's personal attributes has led to some unconventional staff choices. Cantrell expanded the job of the Family Services Center's bus driver, for example, to allow him to work—between driving shifts—as a teaching assistant in the early childhood program. Cantrell recognized this employee as a warm, caring, and intelligent person who, as an African-

American male, could also provide an excellent role model for many children. Cantrell's alertness to staff potential has opened up new career horizons for this man, who has since enrolled in Head Start training and courses at the local community college. Brendza hired as a preschool teacher a woman who had been working as a maid at a ski resort. Despite her lack of previous work with children, the woman's love for children, combined with ongoing training in High/Scope offered by The Center, has made her one of The Center's best teachers.

But understanding and love for children are not always enough. Program directors must recognize, for example, when families need the help of an experienced, professional therapist more than that of a well-meaning home visitor. Also, the use of paraprofessionals is limited in states that have strict requirements for early childhood teachers that may include a specific number of formal college credits.

While each program has formal job descriptions, flexible, easy-going attitudes of staff contribute to programs' success. These staff members are not apt to say, "Sorry, not in my job description." They are willing to do whatever is needed to help a family and run the program successfully. "Do you ever do any tasks not in your job description?" we asked The Center's staff. "All the time," replied one teacher. "Today I oiled the pet pig. He has dry skin."

Training and Staff Development

Each day, a family support home visitor may walk into someone's house and be confronted by illness, illiteracy, child neglect, substandard housing, unemployment, and a furnace low on oil in the middle of a cold January. Immediately, the home visitor needs to ask herself a range of questions: What agencies need to be called? How can I teach the parents to negotiate their way through these agencies? Is emergency medical care needed? She then drives on to the next family and confronts a totally different set of problems and personalities. How does a person learn to do all this?

According to the staff of our three programs, it takes training, training, and more training. This is especially the case for paraprofessionals, but it is certainly not limited to them. Many professionals need new training to "undo" their formal education. This is the case, for example, for teachers who were taught that what goes on in children's homes is of secondary importance to their education, or for social service workers used to addressing only a family's problems and not its strengths. Several issues that family support workers must now deal with may not even have been realities when the worker first received training and education. Working with families with an HIV positive member or educating children prenatally exposed to crack are new challenges that require new skills.

All three programs employ at least several of the following measures to advance staff training:

- paying for courses at local community colleges or universities
- providing for senior staff or outside professionals to conduct in-house training for teachers and parent educators
- sending staff to conferences
- having staff observe program supervisors in their interactions with families and offering suggestions for improvements
- holding joint training sessions with local social service agencies

Such ongoing training has meant a low staff turnover rate for all three programs. However, of the few staff members at each program who have left their jobs, most were paraprofessionals who benefited so much from their job experience and their on-the-job training that they decided to return to school fulltime to pursue teaching degrees or other education.

At Early Education Services, funds to provide staff training were written into the discretionary part of the Comprehensive Child Development Program (CCDP) grant and are utilized by staff who serve participants covered by the grant. This money funds in-house training led by an EES staff member three times a month; tuition payments for staff members without an associate's degree to attend the local community college; and a workshop series on such topics as child abuse or developmental delays in adults conducted several times a year by outside experts. By devoting so much funding to training, Jerald is able to hire people on the basis of promise, rather than a proven track record. "I wanted people who came in with a clean slate because this is a new field," she says.

EES' other federally funded programs, Even Start and Follow Through, also have extensive training components. Educational consultants come to Brattleboro periodically to work with Follow Through teachers, and specialists in family literacy provide training to the Even Start staff.

One-on-one training is an effective way to give a staff person concrete suggestions for improving her effectiveness. Typically, a senior staff person will accompany the home visitor on a site visit, observe her interactions with the family, and then offer recommendations. Through supervision combined with mentoring, staff members get the individual attention they need to hone their skills. Family support staff, especially those that work in the field (and, thus, largely on their own) value time spent in meetings with other staffers brainstorming about families' needs and how best to provide services.

From the early stages of its development, The Center was committed to hiring local residents for its teaching staff, in order both to build a staff that understood the community and to augment the job pool in a region hit hard by unemployment. The question was how to find a sufficient number of qualified people in the vicinity of Leadville, an isolated mountain community with a small population. Training was the answer. Because of severe economic distress, most residents of the area qualified for training under the federally funded Job Training and Partnership Act (JTPA). At the behest of The Center, Colorado Mountain College applied for JTPA funds, which it used to provide classes for the seventeen people who had applied for teaching positions at The Center. The trainees then spent ninety hours at The Center as teachers-in-training. At the conclusion of their six-hundred-hour training program, Brendza was free to decide which of the trainees, none of whom had been guaranteed a job, she would offer permanent positions. She ended up hiring twelve of the seventeen.

The Center's training efforts are primarily directed at teaching the High/Scope curriculum to teachers. Brendza herself was trained at High/Scope headquarters in Ypsilanti, Michigan, and returns periodically for further training. She trains her staff according to their different levels of prior experience in teaching High/Scope. That is, teachers who are new to the High/Scope curriculum receive more intensive training compared to those more familiar with it. Colorado Mountain College also offers its own teacher training courses. By enrolling in these courses, Center staff members earn the academic credits to advance beyond the teacher's aide level and, thus, to increase their salaries and benefits. Brendza's method of evaluating her teaching staff is, in effect, another training mechanism: She evaluates only four teachers a year in order to allow herself the time to work intensely with each teacher to strengthen her teaching skills.

The Family Services Center has a more professional staff (many with college and master's degrees) than the other two programs and relies more on training provided by Head Start and the school district on early childhood education, parent involvement, and other educational topics. A member of the education staff told us, "I feel supported by the program. I'm being sent to a family literacy conference this coming week. When the funds are available and when it's feasible, it has worked out."

Compensating and Supporting Staff

The organization of the programs within the school system affects the way staff are compensated. The Family Services Center, for example, is a program formally under the Alachua County school district's early childhood unit, which, in turn, is part of the division of elementary education. Consequently, staff members are hired through the district and are paid within the established salary structure for all school employees. EES, by contrast, is organized as a composite of grant-funded programs, with the school functioning as the administrator of these grants. Its employees are not unionized like the rest of the Brattleboro school district's staff. Home visitors, however, earn the same salary as teacher's aides in the schools, while EES administrators earn less than their district counterparts. The Center is organized as a separate nonprofit agency of the school district. Its distinct status gives The Center the freedom to establish its own salary structure. The Center's paraprofessionals earn more than their equivalents hired to work in the district's schools.

Although our three programs are all sponsored by school districts, they are not funded by them. Rather, like most family support programs, they depend on funding patched together from a variety of local, state, federal, and foundation sources. Sustaining their organization on grant funding is a challenge for all three programs. A considerable amount of time is required to identify possible funding sources and to write grant proposals. Moreover, only a portion of all proposals will be successful. The uncertainty of ongoing, long-term funding makes it difficult to hire and retain staff. At the Family Services Center, for example, Cantrell had to let a social worker go when grant funds were cut; two other staff members left for jobs with more stable funding.

A further complication is the impossibility of replacing a staff member who leaves toward the end of a grant, because a position would be open for only a few months. Unless replacement money can be found, the program must continue to function with fewer staff. This problem requires project directors to be creative with financing. For example, many positions at the Family Services Center are funded by more than one source, as described in Chapter 7. In addition to patching together funds for staff, program directors must also give their staff professional support if they expect to retain them. Management styles and techniques are a crucial component of this system of professional support.

Judie Jerald, Linda Cantrell, and Kathy Brendza have similar management styles—all are open and consultative with staff. An underlying philosophy guides their work: If you expect your staff to empower participants, your staff must be empowered in its own work situation.

Jerald credits her experience as a group leader in the social work field with forming her consultative style. In keeping with that experience, she holds regular staff meetings to discuss individual cases, as well as program strategies. She also encourages staff to give her honest feedback about the way EES is managed. Brendza has very high expectations for her staff but does not want to use a tight rein to achieve them. She and her three assistant directors allow The Center teachers to make decisions about the children and classroom activities and work schedules among themselves. At the Family Services Center, Cantrell espouses an "open door policy that's going to kill me at some point, because I'm never going to get any paperwork done. But I'm open all the time to them [staff]; I love for them to come up with ideas. They come up with a lot better solutions to problems than I can, given the multitude of things we're doing here."

A spirit of openness, shared by staff and management, nurtures innovation. One EES administrator reflects on her experience with the staff, saying, "We would bump into each other at the copier many, many times during the day. We'd see a bunch of kids through the window doing nothing. So we would start talking about play groups and our ideas would just build. We ended with a summer camp last year for a lot of kids just because of that spontaneous discussion."

High pressure atmospheres and low salaries associated with family support work require management to continually look for ways to lessen the staff's burdens. Monthly peer support groups and office retreats are vehicles for preventing staff burnout. At EES, Parents As Teachers home visitors get the summers off and can stay at home with their own children on the public schools' "snow days." "It's those kinds of benefits that make it worthwhile for a woman to take the low pay and high stress," says EES' early education specialist, Dot Marsden. Family Services Center's staff has an adjustable forty hour work week: Conducting home visits at night or on the weekend means taking some time off during weekdays.

BUILDING STRONG RELATIONSHIPS BETWEEN STAFF AND FAMILIES

There are no two ways about it: To be successful, family support programs must have staff that can build trusting relationships with families worn out by and wary of organizations that say they want to "help." Above all else, family support workers need to be nonjudgmental and optimistic. As one Family Services Center education specialist puts it, staff members must believe that even people who are considered "losers and quitters" can become winners, if someone cares enough. Yet, attempts to exert a positive influence must be subtle, says an EES home visitor. "You don't go into someone else's home and impose your sense of the world on them," she explains. But subtlety does not come easily to all family support staff. Diane Kolson, an EES home visitor, recalls that it took her some time to develop the right approach:

> First of all, I learned that I had judgments. You know, I thought I was this wonderful open person that could go in and be right there, at whatever level these people were, and I learned that I did have judgments. I really had to work on their point of view, working from their intuition about what they needed, not what I thought they needed for their children.

The parent educators in the three programs strive to achieve the appropriate, and very delicate, balance between being a guide as well as a friend to the families with whom they work. As a parent in an EES program says:

> I've wanted to do some pretty outrageous things that I probably couldn't do, but my home visitor never laughed at me and said, "Oh, come on. You'll never be able to do that." She stood right beside me and if I fell down, she was there to help me get back up and try something different.

It can be difficult, however, for staff to sustain friendly feelings toward parents who exhibit behavior that is inconsistent with healthy parenting. Teachers at The Center report that such situations cause lapses in their efforts to be nonjudgmental. One teacher in the program says that most parents fail to give their children enough quality time or to provide appropriate discipline; it then falls to The Center staff to meet these unfulfilled needs. Staff members' conflicts over supporting a parent while protecting a child in this kind of situation pales by comparison to the conflict many feel when they must report cases of suspected child abuse to the authorities. EES home visitors say they experience real discomfort in this situation. As advocates for parents in dealing with the social service and legal systems, they are obliged to help the parents through the legal process initiated by the allegation of abuse. Yet, ironically, sometimes it is they who set that process in motion.

The willingness of a highly committed staff to go out of its way to help families may, as an unintended consequence, actually discourage a family's moves toward independence. Staff members often drive parents to appointments, help them fill out forms, and talk to their doctors and their children's teachers. It is crucial, therefore, that the staff be trained to model behavior that will promote the independence of participants in the program. First, parents need to be shown how to deal with agencies, doctors, and the school system; then they must be required to take on those tasks themselves. Allowance is made in all three programs for parents to experience an initial stage of dependence on the staff; if they have to be dependent on someone, directors say, family support staff is preferable to someone who may be a negative influence. Furthermore, as Jerald points out, dependence is the precursor to autonomy: "You have to be dependent. You're going to crawl before you walk. You'll learn to walk if you're nurtured and loved enough. It will happen."

Lessons for Practitioners

The success of a family support program is critically dependent on the quality of its staff. Most family support workers—professionals and paraprofessionals alike—are highly committed to the families and communities they serve. It is crucial that managers work hard to empower their staff by creating a work culture that centers around trust and full participation. The fact that at the three sites staff turnover has been low is a clear indication that the right people have been hired and that they are treated well. We recommend that program directors take the following steps in order to hire and retain the right staff:

1. *Develop multiple criteria for hiring staff.* Directors should not be afraid to hire people more on the basis of their personal qualities than on the experience listed on their resumes. The hiring process is time consuming but rewarding when personable and quick-learning individuals join the staff. It is worth taking the time to interview candidates in depth and solicit the opinions of other staff members. Consider criteria such as attitudes toward children and parents, willingness to work flexibly, disposition toward home visits, and ability to work as part of a team.

2. *Make pre- and in-service training a priority.* Training and staff development opportunities are a good way to build staff expertise. They also convey to the staff that its work is valued highly. This is an important message for employees who receive low pay and shoulder tremendous responsibility. Consider training in early childhood and parenting education, as well as outreach and recruitment strategies, education for children with special needs, record keeping and information management, and ways to work with parents with special problems (such as lack of self-esteem). The staff also needs supervision of its

relationships with program participants. Guidance, especially for home visitors, should be provided for dealing with the dilemmas often created by the intensity of relationships between staff and family.

3. *Exercise creative leadership by remaining open to staff ideas and letting the staff make decisions.* Family support programs thrive on team relationships: Staff meetings provide an opportunity for many individual perspectives to create a whole that is greater than the sum of its parts. An environment where staff ideas are implemented—through individual or group decision making—stimulates ongoing innovation and program development. Set up regular mechanisms to receive staff input, such as staff meetings, informal talks at brown bag lunches, yearly planning retreats, and performance evaluations.

4. *Make "care for the caregiver" a routine aspect of program operations.* Most important is to develop good benefits and flexibility for all positions. Remember that members of the staff have families, too; they should not be allowed to burn themselves out helping other families at the expense of their own. Peer support groups, stress management workshops, and office retreats are other ways to help the staff balance the many demands of working with children and families.

7 Funding Family Support Programs

The cost of investing in children and families is insignificant compared to what it will be tomorrow if uncertainty and inaction continue to guide our policies.

National Commission on Children (1991:372)

The three programs in this study are responsible for their own fundraising and continuously need to adjust their program mission to match their funding resources. Such programs face a range of fiscal challenges as they grow, namely:

- securing start-up funds
- managing diverse funding streams
- making the transition from short-term grants to stable funding
- securing adequate funds for all the different components

Starting a Program Involves Creative Entrepreneurship

In their search for funds, the directors of the three programs in our study combine strategy, risk-taking, and asset-building—qualities that allowed them to start up and, later, to expand their operations. After securing core support, the program directors used this support to attract new funds. Superintendent Jim McCabe of The Center believes that locating start-up money requires an entrepreneurial attitude. "You've got to be able to go out and beat the bushes," he says, "and get people to offer money or offer services or whatever it is they can do." Table 7 (p. 76) shows each program's funding sources and total funds for 1991–1992.

Early Education Services

Developing creative, high-profile strategies to win funding from community resources is a key factor in establishing core support for programs. EES began as a town-funded Parents As Teachers program. School officials in Brattleboro organized an aggressive public relations campaign to influence town representatives to vote funds for Parents As Teachers. This program was presented as a special item in the town budget, separate from the school budget, but to be administered by the

Table 7 Sources of Funding

	Program		
	Early Education Services	*The Center*	*Family Services Center*
Funds for 1991–1992	$1.1 million	$600,000	$1.1 million
Sample of funding source			
Foundations	✓	✓	✓
Town or county funds	✓	✓	In-kind contribution
State family support program	✓		✓
State funds for preschool	✓	✓	✓
State school-linked service program			✓
Head Start		✓	✓
Head Start Demonstration Grant	✓		✓
Even Start	✓		✓
Follow-Through	✓		
School/Family Partnership Grant	✓		
Community Development Block Grant	✓	✓	
Medicaid Reimbursement			✓

school district. Although the town did not allocate the entire amount requested, its grant of $50,000 a year provided the leverage the district's personnel needed to get additional foundation money to start operations. The town's support also created a base to bring in state and federal grants to make Parents As Teachers more comprehensive in its family services, and to create the umbrella organization known as EES.

Since fundraising is usually facilitated by local commitment to a project, program directors must make communities aware of the benefits of family support service. Judie Jerald of EES and her colleagues show town representatives that their $50,000 yearly investment in PAT brings close to a million dollars in other grant funds to the town and county. Thus, says a former PAT administrator, the program is able to convince local politicians of its value "where it counts most, in the pocketbook." A symbiosis has been created: State and federal grants have provided the leverage to win renewed town funding for Parents As Teachers each year.

The Center

Designed as a daycare center and early childhood program, The Center in Leadville required funding and substantial resources for a suitable building. Superintendent Jim McCabe had an empty 30,000 square foot elementary school available to house The Center, but the building needed extensive renovations. These renovations became the centerpiece of The Center's initial funding strategy. McCabe convinced the school board to turn the building over to The Center, along with a loan of $40,000 to begin asbestos removal, repairs, and structural modifications required to make the building accessible to the handicapped. Additional funds for facility improvements were secured from a federal Community Development Block Grant ($140,000) and from the Lake County government ($40,000) (McCabe, 1992:7).

Family Services Center

As a "one-stop shop," the Family Services Center has relied from the outset on participating state and county agencies to support the program, mainly by providing staff. Nevertheless, the school district had to raise funds initially to lease portable structures to house the Family Services Center and add staff positions. The way it went about securing these funds serves as an example of both entrepreneurship and foresight. Superintendent Douglas Magann instructed his project development staff to look for appropriate grants to fund early childhood intervention programs. When they failed to find any, they looked further and discovered a state-funded interagency grant for providing services to middle school students. Not one to let an opportunity pass, Magann applied for the grant and won it. The Family Services Center thus began as a program for middle school students, but over time it has secured grants to serve younger children.

The initial state grant, a little over $100,000, was important because it allowed the Family Services Center to position itself well within the movement toward school-based service integration, and to secure additional state and federal grants to support expansion. Both Magann and top school district officials were sure that prevention programs were important to state-level policy makers and that it was only a matter of time before funds would be earmarked for early childhood programs. And they were right. Within a year of opening its doors, the Family Services Center was able to apply successfully for early childhood education grants, including the state's Florida First Start and the federal Even Start program. This allowed the Family Services Center to offer parenting skills and family literacy programs to families with children from birth to seven years of age. Today about three-fourths of the families enrolled in its programs, excluding the clinic, are families with young children; the rest have children in elementary school.

State funds, from education and social services departments, contribute to the advancement of early childhood education and family support programs. While these funds are more stable for preschool and parenting education programs, they are less certain from year to year for comprehensive family services. This is not surprising given that such initiatives are still in their infancy, and as with many new policies and programs, have to overcome a resistance to change. Programs, therefore, need to develop a strategy of seeking funds from different sources.

Helping Programs Expand through Diverse Funding

"Diversity is the key here if we're going to survive," says Judie Jerald about EES' funding sources. Comprehensive programs for children and families generally rely on multiple and creative funding: No one source can support the range of services these programs deliver. Seeking grants from diverse sources is a strategy common to all three programs, and each has been successful in obtaining federal, state, and foundation funds. "There may not be monies available from one source. So, we just keep aggressively pursuing from every source to pull the program together," says Linda Eldridge, assistant superintendent in Gainesville. "....We are people who go after grants at the national level and we've been real successful. We constantly are looking for ways to meet the program's needs, and I don't think that will end." Her statement, made at a time when Florida state education funds were being cut, reflects the energy and optimism with which funding is—and must be—pursued. With several sources of funding, a family support program has a safety net; if a grant is not renewed, a program can continue to operate on other resources. "We've got it so spread out that we could pull a little bit from here and little bit from there, and I think, weather the storm," says Linda Cantrell of the Family Services Center.

How does diversity in funding help a program grow? Among other things, it increases the likelihood of obtaining grants that will enable a program to offer continuity of services for children, creation of new services for parents, and staff positions to deliver key program components. For example, by securing more grants, Early Education Services has expanded its original infant and toddler program to one that serves children through the third grade. These grants have also enabled EES to increase its scope of parent services. The original town-funded Parents As Teachers program served children birth to age three, and offered some parenting skills classes. The state-funded Parent-Child Centers added parent support groups to the PAT program, and the Early Education Initiative (also a state program) added services to children ages four and five. The federal funds for Even Start, Follow Through, and the Comprehensive Child Development Program (CCDP) grant enabled EES to offer services for children up to age seven, as well as adult education, parent involvement in schools, health and mental health counseling, employment training, and a fathers' support group.

Diverse funding sources can also be combined to support core services and staff positions. Cantrell often speaks about "hybrid" arrangements at the Family Services Center. For example, one of the program's portable units houses the adult education computer lab. The facility, its two teachers, and two aides are supported by a combination of funds: from Chapter 1, Head Start, Even Start, and the Florida Department of Education. Staff positions for health services are put together creatively from the following resources: State Full Service School grant, State Supplemental School Health grant, Medicaid reimbursement, and unpaid nursing student interns from the University of Florida.

Additional funds to a core funding base make it possible to strengthen existing staff positions by extending the hours of part-time staff and increasing salary rates. Early Education Services combines different programs, some more fully funded than others, and arranges for the more solvent programs to contract services from Parents As Teachers, which is underfunded. This arrangement "probably helped PAT to survive," says Judie Jerald. It also enabled her to increase the wages of home visitors. The Parents As Teachers program also runs two state-funded programs: the Parent-Child Center and the Early Education Initiative (EEI) preschool. The EEI preschool has expanded mainly by serving families eligible under CCDP and Even Start funding. Similarly, Follow Through money goes to Parents As Teachers to administer the preschool to kindergarten transition initiative; in return, PAT home visitors spend five percent of their time working for Follow Through participants.

Managing Diverse Funding

One downside to the mosaic approach to funding is that each funding stream has its own eligibility requirements; some families qualify for services under some grants, others under other grants. Eligibility for many programs, for example, is based less on a family's overall needs than on a child's age. The Family Services Center serves a low-income population with children of mixed age groups, ranging from birth through the elementary grades. At the time of our fieldwork in April 1992, renewed funding from the state Full Service School grant was uncertain. Its potential loss was more likely to affect participating families than the program itself. "When you're working with people you want to keep the families tied in," says Cantrell. "The sad thing, if the Full Service School money fails, is that there are 80 families tied into that project. Now the federal grant we're going after would help keep the personnel here, but it has a prekindergarten focus. So unless those families have a prekindergarten child, it's going to be real hard. So, that's what's sad for me, because many are making progress and I don't want to say goodbye." Fortunately, the state reallocated funds for the Full Service Schools program in 1993–1994, enabling the Family Services Center to receive increased funding.

At EES, diverse funding highlights the tension between universal and targeted services. Parents As Teachers was designed as a universal program that would serve all parents, but subsequent grants to EES specify that the use of funds be restricted to at-risk families. This stipulation has met with some resistance from school authorities. The Follow Through program, for example, operates in classrooms where 60 percent of children are eligible for free or reduced-cost lunches. It is designed to consolidate gains made in Head Start and other early education programs by providing extra classroom resources to at-risk children in kindergarten through the third grade. Interventions included in the program are: access to health, nutrition, and other needed services, and activities involving parents in their children's education. Follow Through also offers parent workshops for its participants.

School administrators wanted these open to all parents, regardless of income. A compromise was arranged; workshops are now open to all, but transportation and child care arrangements are available only to Follow Through parents.

Different funding streams also require staff members to keep track of what services they can offer to each family under which grants. Serving families from two funding streams with different resources requires careful bookkeeping, as well as clear boundaries. One EES home visitor says, "Sometimes I know I find myself in a home and stop for a second and ask, 'Who am I? What is my hat here? And what can I offer these people?' For Parents As Teachers, we can't offer all of the services or the money that the Windham County Family Support Program [funded by CCDP] does."

MAKING THE TRANSITION FROM SOFT MONEY TO HARD MONEY

Policy analysts Farrow and Joe (1992:63–67) distinguish three basic types of funding strategies: using core program funding to support basic functions or activities; redirecting existing funds to allocate available resources more efficiently; and maximizing the use of federal funds, especially Medicaid. Each of the programs in our study has core support from local sources, whether in the form of town funds (Early Education Services), redeployed staff (Family Services Center), or sliding scale fees (The Center). Building on these cores, they have secured additional resources, which, in some cases, have put them on the road to more stable funding. According to Lake County Superintendent Jim McCabe, the hardest part in The Center's fundraising experience was making the transition from soft money (time limited grants) to hard money (continuous and more secure resources).

When The Center was first launched, McCabe and Center director Kathy Brendza each spent about 40 percent of their time raising money. "But we also realized that you can't run a center like this on soft money," McCabe says, "on money that you continually have to go out and write grants [for]." At issue was not only the staff's time and energy, but also the stability of the institution. The Center's evolution depended, in part, on getting as much hard money as possible, so that funds would outlast any major personnel turnover: Some community members expressed concern that The Center's success in obtaining foundation grants has been closely tied to the personalities of McCabe and Brendza, and that, if they leave, funding for the program might disappear. Therefore, hard money became a priority. Currently, The Center receives stable funding (hard money) from these sources:

- Parent contributions in the form of fees for daycare and before- and afterschool care
- Department of Education's Colorado Preschool Project for preschool programs
- Lake County Department of Social Services for single-parent daycare programs
- Department of Education for preschool handicapped children
- Mountain Valley Developmental Center for services to handicapped children
- Head Start for preschool programs

Thanks to its funding from Head Start, The Center has begun operating in the black and is able to pay back the debt incurred in its start-up phase (McCabe, 1992:12). "Enough hard money is available to make up 90 percent of the operating costs," says McCabe. The remainder of the money must be raised from foundations and time-limited state grants.

A related issue is that multifaceted family support programs may acquire hard money for some services, but not for others. For example, The Center has been able to secure hard money for its early childhood program but has had less success raising funds to strengthen its family support component. Proposals for an Even Start grant and a state Family Center grant were turned down. Kathy Brendza surmises that previous fundraising success may be working against The Center, by giving potential funders the impression that it has enough resources. She is currently raising funds to add new services to the family support component, including a family preservation project, fathering classes, parenting classes for parents of teenagers, and recreational programs that involve the family as an entire unit.

With a combination of redeployed staff and Medicaid reimbursements to support family-focused comprehensive services, the Family Services Center is successfully beginning to substitute hard money for soft. Both of these funding sources are more stable than the state and federal demonstration project grants that the Family Services Center has received to support its work. In fact, the Family Services Center has outlived some state grant programs that have been cut. It has also seen one of its grant-funded programs rotate in and out of state budgets. Staff members who are paid out of the budgets of their respective agencies but assigned to the Family Services Center serve as an in-kind source of core support. Medicaid reimbursements also fill an important gap in funding the salaries of an on-site health practitioner and a mental health specialist, both of whom depend on state grants. While Medicaid is not the primary source of funding for these positions, it is an essential component of it.

The long-term viability of Early Education Services is challenged by the need to constantly renew funding and by the ever-present reality that federal grants may come to an end. Jerald admits that downsizing is a possibility. "We might have to get smaller if something happens with the CCDP funding," she says, "but we can survive with the variety of other funding sources we have." While Jerald has successfully tapped several federal funding streams, and used these funds to expand family support services beyond Brattleboro to other school districts, she still faces the challenge of securing more stable alternatives to ensure continuous and comprehensive family support.

One step EES has taken is to affiliate with the state's Success By Six initiative, which encourages cost-effective collaboration among education and health service providers to prepare children for school. In Brattleboro, this initiative has sparked many activities. Cross-training for agencies using a video that documents services available in the community has been accomplished. Agencies participating in the initiative meet monthly to do case management for teen parents whom they serve. Plans are also underway to co-locate human service personnel in schools, and to coordinate interagency preventive health care and developmental screenings. Finally, efforts are being made to strengthen community-wide support of the readiness goal. A committee of townspeople has been formed to identify businesses that are safe and friendly for children, to refurbish playgrounds, and to sponsor family recreational activities.

SCHOOLS AND FAMILY SUPPORT PROGRAMS: *Mutually Beneficial Funding Relationships*

The relationship between the programs in our study and their local school districts sometimes causes public misperceptions about the programs' funding base. These need to be corrected by the programs' directors. School support (in-kind and financial) and school personnel have, indeed, played large roles in getting the family support programs off the ground. But none of the programs receives funding for operating costs from its local school district. The Center, for example, prides itself on not relying on local tax dollars for any operating costs. Funds to cover its $600,000 yearly budget must be raised independently (McCabe, 1992:11). Half the operating costs are covered by daycare fees paid by parents, and the other half by fundraising from external sources, such as state and foundation grants.

Yet, a perception exists among residents in Leadville that local school funds are going to The Center. This confusion has arisen, in part, because the district loaned start-up money to The Center, and continues to provide routine maintenance to its building. Residents form their opinion based on ongoing capital costs, "donated" to The Center in the form of minor building repairs and maintenance, rather than on operating costs. According to McCabe, the district would have to maintain the school building whether The Center occupied it or not, but many residents view upkeep as a specific local tax contribution to The Center. It should be pointed out that even if the district were willing to fund the full operating costs of The Center, Kathy Brendza would be tempted to decline the offer. The Center now enjoys a degree of flexibility as a "franchise" of the school district that is beneficial to the program which, she says, would be lost: "If we took district money, then we would have to comply with all sorts of regulations that right now we don't have to comply with."

Some school officials in Brattleboro, convinced that an early childhood program is integral to the school's educational mission, consider it time to fold Parents As Teachers into the local school budget. One PAT administrator, however, does not agree to a school-funded strategy: Putting the program in direct competition with other school programs would make its funding more tenuous, rather than less. She maintains that town officials, who have an interest in the jobs and economic impact of EES' programs, are more likely to provide continuous and adequate funding than school officials, who must choose among many underfunded programs.

School districts have made valuable in-kind contributions on a regular basis, as shown in Table 7.1. Occasionally, a school district makes a one-time offer that substantially alters the course of a program's development. Such was the case when the Brattleboro school district decided to fund PAT to hire a grant writer for the CCDP grant. The funds secured by the writer led to the formation of EES.

Family support programs benefit from district resources, but the district also benefits from the programs. Many service components have resulted from collaborations between programs and school districts that respond to their respective needs. In Brattleboro, an Infant-Toddler Child Care Center was established jointly by and at the regional vocational high school and EES' Windham County Family Support Program. The school provides the space, its upkeep, and a coordinating teacher, while EES equips the center, pays for two caregivers, and provides technical assistance and training. Although students enrolled in the Windham County Family Support Program are given priority, the child care center is open to other high school parents as well.

Table 7.1 **Regular School Contributions to Family Support Programs**

School Contribution	**Program** *Early Education Services*	*The Center*	*Family Services Center*
Building space and land	✓	✓	
Grant proposal research and development			✓
Financial management	✓	✓	✓
Teaching staff assigned to program			✓

In exchange for the school contributions, family support programs try to "give" to the district by jointly sponsoring activities with other school programs. The Center, for example, offers high school students—a number of them male—the opportunity to work after school as paid teacher aides. One parent commends this initiative for providing students with an opportunity to learn the value of responsibility and to begin thinking about career choices. "It's been impressive to me to see those high school students working with the children," he says. "And I know The Center has affected numbers of high school students' career paths because of that experience." The three programs have developed creative arrangements to link themselves to school activities. Among them are: discussing third grade assignments in an adult education classroom, offering child care for high school students, and providing a school-home liaison for K–3 students.

STRATEGIES FOR SUCCESSFUL FUNDRAISING

"Funding is the most difficult issue that you deal with," says The Center's Jim McCabe. His views resonate with other program administrators who identify money matters as a major concern. Yet, despite the uncertainty and risk involved in locating funds, the three directors remain undaunted. They all share the optimistic view that successful fundraising is within reach and work hard to prove the point. They also believe that sooner, rather than later, policy makers will come to support—and fund—prevention programs, which are less costly in financial and human terms than later interventions. In the meantime, as EES' Judie Jerald says, "we have to be creative and stay on it."

While the key component of a successful fundraising strategy is to develop quality programs worthy of support, these three programs also attract and sustain funding by building local commitment, cultivating community support, writing effective grant proposals, and publicizing their work.

Local commitment

The start-up of a family support program is made much easier if there is local commitment to the program, says Laurie Emel, former director of the Parents As Teachers program. Of the three programs, the only town to make an ongoing financial contribution to EES' family support services is Brattleboro. Local funds are especially important because state and federal funds will not be available to set up programs in every town that needs them. From her own experience, Emel is convinced that programs such as Parents As Teachers, that start on a small scale, can ultimately make a large impact—and solidify local financial support—on other communities by providing affordable models for replication. "It isn't realistic for this and that small town of Vermont to muster the resources to have a really blue chip intervention program with the resources of the Windham County Family Support Program," she says. "They [state officials] are very interested in Parents As Teachers because it serves everyone and is run on a shoestring budget." Legislators and town fathers are likely to invest "in something that has a good payoff because it heads off problems," says Emel. To build support for a program, she also advocates launching a community campaign that focuses on the pride a community can take in creating "a child friendly and family supportive community."

Community support

Local agencies should work together closely to augment the range of services that can be provided to families. Through a system of referrals, contracted services, co-located staff, and in-kind contributions, agencies can bring together a wide variety of family-focused services. The Center, for example, has maximized locally available resources to offer nonacademic services that were not available through education funds. Comprehensive care for children—especially health services, developmental screening, and protective services—and programs in adult education and parenting are offered through local agencies that either send representatives to The Center on a regular basis or are on call to provide services when The Center needs them. Thus, The Center has become a hub for family, child, and community interaction.

Grant writing

Attracting sufficient funds to sustain a family support program requires an ongoing grant writing effort, a tedious and time-consuming, but essential, task. Program directors must find ways of efficiently allocating scarce staff time to this endeavor and are well advised to draw on any available resources in the school district or the community at large. Preparing proposals demands much of the director's own energy, at the same time as he or she is running the program. "It would be neat not to have to worry about competing (for funds) all the time," says Family Services Center director Linda Cantrell.

Some school districts help program staff write grant proposals and identify future funding sources. Cantrell, for example, has access to the services of her large school district's Project Development Office, which reviews incoming requests for proposals and notifies school departments when they might be eligible for specific grants. Judie Jerald, however, operating in a small rural district with fewer resources, runs her own one-person grant seeking operation. "I think the money is out there," she says. "What worries me about the resources is having the people, the staff to go after it...I think it would be true for any family support program because they're all going to be looking for money all over the place. You've got to bring in a lot of different resources to make something like this work. So, you've got to have people who know money, who understand budgets, fundraising, accounting...It's important." When Jerald got wind of the CCDP request for proposals, she successfully advocated for the school board to provide funds to hire a professional grant writer for the project.

Publicity

Program directors have to be creative in getting the word out about their program's accomplishments. The Family Services Center is a showcase program that is visited frequently by school and government officials from Florida and other states. Local newspapers and national publications have featured in-depth articles on both Early Education Services and The Center, thanks to the efforts of these programs' directors. This visibility helps programs retain their sources of support, as well as attract new ones.

Lessons for Practitioners

Stable, secure funding is crucial to the success of a family support program. Directors must be alert and imaginative in determining how to present their programs in ways that will interest a range of funders.

Above all, a successful fundraising effort requires tenacity. We recommend the following measures to build program funding:

1. *Be creative and tenacious in pursuing funding.* Start-up funds for family support programs are the foundation for securing later support. Gaining access to this initial resource requires not only gathering information about the community and developing a research base to support a program's plan of action, but it also requires advocacy, especially when funds are sought locally. Program planners must be able to persuade a school board or town officials that their program is worth trying out.

When external sources of funding are sought, it is important to identify those that most closely match the program's mission. Information about the sources and goals of private foundation funding can be obtained through grant registers found at local public or college libraries, or purchased from the publishers. Local offices of the state departments of education, health, and social services, possess information about state-funded programs and, in some cases, federal programs. A list of federal funds is found in the Catalogue of Federal Domestic Assistance of the General Services Administration.

2. *Investigate school district resources.* School districts can often provide in-kind support such as space, office equipment, grant writing assistance, and business management services. School authorities can also sometimes be persuaded to reallocate a portion of education funds from federal and state sources, such as Chapter 1 and drug prevention money, to assist a family support program.

3. *Carefully build school district support for programs.* If a school district provides services to a family support program, it should be well rewarded by the benefits associated with the program, namely, a more coherent system of services for students and their families. A good family support program can integrate what was, before its arrival, a maze of fragmented services offered by the schools. The school's less efficient use of services can be transformed into a well-functioning system that will, undoubtedly, be valued and supported by the district. Use these achievements to solidify continuing school support and to solicit new funding to fill gaps in the current service delivery.

4. *Extend the base of program support beyond the school system.* Community agencies that work with the same base of local families often appreciate the helping hand a family support program gives to their clients. A program director would be well advised to seek the endorsement of these agencies in drafting grant proposals and become their partner in advocating for a better system of services for all children and families in the community. Other strategies for building this

support include sharing space, facilities, and staff training, and co-sponsoring activities.

5. *Involve participants as program advocates.* Participants are important resources of a program. They can serve as spokespersons in meetings with program funders, or share their program experiences in interviews with the media. As advocates, participants can have a hand in sustaining the program and even helping it expand to offer services to more people in the community. The opportunity to take on this responsibility builds their self-esteem and allows them to be not only recipients but also contributors to a community's family support services. Thus, the relationship between program and participants becomes a reciprocal one. Cultivate opportunities for participants to give testimony before the school board or the town meeting; include them as key informants for a news article or radio talk show.

6. *Search out diverse funding sources and be prepared to manage them.* Securing funds from diverse sources enables a program to develop new activities and support new staff positions. Since it ties the program into different funding streams, diversity also allows for continuous operations, despite flux situations in short-term funding cycles that can, otherwise, debilitate a program. Program directors need to commit a considerable portion of their time to researching the wide range of funding sources in order to identify those that are most compatible with their programs' mission. Once funds are secured, the directors must set up clear systems to manage the eligibility criteria and conditions set by the different sources. However, directors can sometimes convince funders on the merits of flexible funding, for example, to support heterogeneous classrooms or to open parenting workshops for all parents and not just for at-risk families.

7. *Set as a goal making the transition from soft to hard money.* Family support programs operate in an uncertain environment when they are funded by soft money. In order to continue to stay in business, program directors will have to work at finding stable sources of support. This objective may be achieved by successfully advocating for local school or town funds, entering into collaborative arrangements with community agencies, and pursuing federal entitlement programs. In addition, program directors should educate policy makers on the need for stable and flexible funding for comprehensive child and family services. By documenting in evaluations or annual reports the operational experiences of their program, and by participating in state and national conferences attended by policy makers, program directors are in the best position to make the case for long-term financial support.

8 Continuing Challenges

We have emphasized the importance of a community-by-community approach in ensuring the well-being of families and improving the life chances of our children and youth. However, responsibility for implementing these strategies cannot be assigned to a particular agency or level of government; it is shared by our entire nation. State government in particular has a crucial role to play.

Council of Chief State School Officers (1992:17)

The three programs in this study exemplify heroic efforts to integrate a range of resources and services for families in their communities. We call their efforts heroic because they have been undertaken in a service environment where bureaucratic structures divide rather than bridge policies and programs for children and families. Among the conditions these programs have confronted are:

- a fragmented service delivery system
- regulatory policies that inhibit, rather than facilitate, local collaboration
- categorical funding streams
- limited health services for low-income families
- limited technical and financial support to evaluate the full scope of their programs.

Throughout this report we have stressed the benefits that accrue when a family support program is designed and managed at the local level. But it should also be obvious from our description of the financial backing of the three programs—coming, in large part, from the Colorado Preschool Program, Vermont Parent-Child Centers and Early Education Initiative, Florida's Full Service Schools and Supplemental School Health programs—how essential state funding is to their existence. The support a community needs from its state government includes, but is not limited to, money; it also needs state government to support school-linked services by providing technical assistance, creating flexible funding streams, and easing state regulations and restrictions that hinder collaboration. It is not enough for state policy makers to pay lip service to the benefits of family support programs; they must also facilitate the establishment, expansion, and ongoing success of those programs. In the following pages, we offer recommendations for policy makers, some of them based on examples from Colorado, Florida, and Vermont, others emerging from "gaps" we identified in the course of doing our three case studies. These recommendations are summarized in Table 8 (p. 92) and then discussed in greater detail.

Recommendations for Policy Makers: *Policies that Work in Florida, Colorado, and Vermont*

Provide incentives to better integrate education, health, and social service programs.

The specialized functions of bureaucracies continue to pose a formidable barrier to collaboration. Since a school system is the logical host for a range of social services, policy makers should stipulate that funds from the education and social services departments are coordinated in order to underwrite comprehensive programs. At the very least, states can fund local coordinators to help families gain access to services and to network with community providers to facilitate the process.

- In Florida, Commissioner Betty Castor of the Department of Education successfully advocated for funds from the Full Service School program to be used to integrate education, health, and social services on or near school premises. This effort broadened the Department of Health and Rehabilitative Services' efforts to bring health services to schools through the Supplemental School Health Services. In 1991–1992 twenty-four counties received funding from both sources, enabling them to promote collaboration among local agencies (Harvard Family Research Project, 1992:29–35).
- Colorado's Preschool Program, authorized by Governor Roy Romer, supports integrated early childhood care and education. It provides school districts with the funds to establish their

Table 8 Policy Recommendations for Comprehensive Early Childhood and Family Support Programs

On funding and resources:

- Provide incentives to better integrate education, health, and social service programs
- Establish noncategorical funding
- Create multiyear funding
- Provide in-kind contributions
- Develop a strategic plan to allocate federal funds efficiently
- Establish an information clearinghouse to assist local fundraising

On broadening the scope of existing programs:

- Provide incentives to make parent involvement and family support an integral component of early childhood care and education
- Find new ways to invest in children's health

On governance:

- Encourage mutually beneficial state and local relationships
- Designate responsibility for the welfare of young children
- Examine state regulations to remove policy conflicts

On building institutional capacity:

- Create a long-range plan for the efficient use of funds
- Build the capacity for evaluation
- Provide assistance for staff training

---

own preschool program or to subcontract with existing child care agencies and Head Start. It also encourages interagency linkages for extended daycare services that can be paid for from social services funds, job training funds, and private sources (Colorado House Bill No. 1341).

- Vermont has mandated that Parent Child Centers, local offices of the Human Services Agency, the Department of Education, and other assorted organizations carry out new collaborative efforts. The state will contract with the Parent Child Centers to

> provide case management to move welfare recipients toward self-sufficiency and to offer an array of preemployment services and activities. These agencies will also work together to provide services for handicapped infants, toddlers, and their families. In an effort to establish a direct link between schools and social services, every school principal will be assigned a contact person at the Human Services Agency.

Provide incentives to make parent involvement and family support an integral component of early childhood care and education.

There are several ways that states can make a long-term investment in preventive programs for children to avoid costly social problems later on. They can initiate family support programs that will be implemented by different community-based organizations. They can also build parent involvement and family support activities into legislation creating preschool programs. Recognizing that child development is facilitated by a healthy home-school partnership, the Colorado Preschool Program obligates the programs it funds to set parent involvement as a condition for enrolling a child.

Encourage mutually beneficial state and local relationships.

State backing of family support programs is most effective when it encourages communities to test innovative program approaches, while sustaining program quality. Programs with the flexibility to adapt state rules to community conditions are better able to meet the needs of children and families and prevent participants from falling through the cracks. They can test what works and what does not work. The state can play an important role in providing technical assistance, beginning at the grant planning stage, and in supervising a program to ensure quality services. By observing local programs and learning from their strengths and experiences, the state, in turn, derives information useful in its efforts to replicate promising innovations. The Center receives state funds to host week-long dissemination sessions, at which representatives from other Colorado communities that want to start similar programs can learn how to put the necessary pieces together.

Designate responsibility for the welfare of young children.

Since it can be unclear in the case of any collaborative effort who bears ultimate responsibility for the funds and for the success of the program, state dollars should not be disbursed without strict accountability requirements. A single entity needs to be assigned responsibility at the local level for overseeing the disbursement of funds and ensuring that the program objectives are met. In our three cases, the school districts assumed this accountability function, but that need not be the case in every community. What is essential is that all the parties invested in the welfare of the community's children—parents, local organizations, and state agencies—know exactly where the buck stops.

Create multiyear funding.

Securing stable funding is an overriding concern for all programs. Unfortunately, many early childhood and family support programs depend on funds allocated on a yearly basis. There is no certainty, therefore, that they will have the financial ability to continue operating from one year to the next. The first year of operation is always difficult as administrators try to juggle the start-up activities to operate the program. If, in addition, they have to divert a portion of their energies to locating replacement money for state funding that will expire at the end of the year, their programs can suffer from insufficient attention. Furthermore, the critical first year task of gaining the trust of participants is jeopardized if those participants are uncertain of the program's ongoing existence. Finally, it is hard to hire staff if they cannot be guaranteed long-term jobs. Not many people, especially those who are already employed, are eager to take on a new job with unstable funding.

As an alternative, funding for two to three years (possibly in amounts that decrease each year), gives programs the best opportunity for starting up and building a track record to attract other funding sources. Ideally, such funding is renewable after the initial grant years are up. The Family Services Center's clinic was funded with short-term funds, a six-month grant followed by a renewable one-year grant. Uncertain that the grant would be renewed, the staff had a difficult time planning for the clinic's future. In contrast, EES and The Center have multiyear funding sources that give them the freedom, first, to concentrate on running their programs without concern for the immediate future and, second, to cultivate participants' trust in the services without fear that the programs may not be around to deliver on their promises.

Provide in-kind contributions.

Given the many demands placed on tight state budgets, policy makers should think creatively about what the state can contribute besides money. Possibilities include:

Co-location of Staff: Reassigning state agency positions to family support programs may be a more useful and stable contribution than funds that have to be renewed every year. In addition to saving the program money on wages, this arrangement puts state social service workers in locations that are usually more convenient and attractive to participants than state offices. Thus, co-location should result in more people seeking the service. The Family Services Center is an excellent example of state agencies contributing staff and services to a program.

Provision of Physical Space: Programs are greatly helped by donations of land and buildings owned by the school district. Just as helpful would be the contribution of space in a publicly owned building in the community.

RECOMMENDATIONS FOR POLICY MAKERS: *Policies Useful to Family Support Programs*

Examine state regulations to remove policy conflicts.

Local offices of state agencies have limited discretion to change regulations and alter the status quo of the bureaucracy. These constraints frequently hinder a locality's attempts at collaboration. All too often program directors and staff must rely on their personal networks to effect the rule-bending needed to get services for their participants. If action is taken at the state level to ease state regulations that obstruct collaboration, local efforts will be spared countless ongoing struggles. Areas that often require waivers are: funding categories, confidentiality, eligibility and qualifying criteria, case management, conflicts in scheduling, and length of benefits.

Develop a strategic plan to use federal funds efficiently.

Every state receives formula grants and block grants from the federal government to distribute to organizations for service provision. The block grant most suitable for family support programs is Title XX of the Social Security Act, known as the Social Services Block Grant, provided by the Department of Health and Human Services (HHS), which has used as much as 20 percent of its funding for child care services. Recent years have seen the creation of new federal sources of funds for child care and child-related services that are funnelled through the states. These include the Family Support Act, Title IV-A of the Social Security Act for At-Risk Child Care Program, Child Care Improvement Grants, Child Care Block Grants, and the Individuals with Disabilities Act, which calls for early intervention with children between birth and age two who are experiencing developmental delays. In addition, the Head Start Reauthorization Act provided money to 12 states to use as collaboration grants for Head Start to work more closely with other child-oriented programs (Levy, Kagan, and Copple, 1992:14–15). (In the past, Head Start money always went directly to the local sponsors, rather than going through the state government.)

Making the best use of these funds requires policy makers to develop a strategic plan, since it is not effective to distribute the funds in a piecemeal fashion. Such a plan would require collaboration, long-term vision, and a commitment to serve families in the most comprehensive ways possible.

Establish an information clearinghouse to assist local fundraising.

State government should also function as a clearinghouse for federal sources of funds. By cataloguing funding sources relevant to family support activities, the state provides local programs with enhanced abilities to track down sources of funding. This function, requiring a relatively small effort, could be the state's "leverage" for facilitating its access to federal money. Local programs often lack the personnel or resources to keep abreast of all relevant funding sources, and thus, miss important sources of money hidden away in federal agencies not usually associated with programs for children. The Department of Housing and Urban Development, for example, has funds for child care centers that it channels through the Public Housing Child Care Demonstration Program. Many federal monies go directly to local programs, bypassing state governments, and would not necessarily be identified as part of the state's strategic plan for funding family support activities. The clearinghouse would be instrumental in helping local programs gain access to these funds.

With a new federal administration, it is particularly crucial for states to be on top of federal funding options. Changes in existing sources, as well as new sources of funding, need to be followed closely.

Establish flexible, noncategorical funding.

It is counterproductive for a program to require that an individual fit into a category of need in order to receive services. It is people that must define the need, not the program. Every family has a unique set of capabilities and needs that is in continual flux. What a family needs in December may not be what it needs in May.

The best approach is to release funds noncategorically or in broadly defined categories for communities to spend as they see fit. Broad categories can be specified in terms of age (e.g., spent on children from birth to three) or by status (such as "at risk," with criteria defined by the community). This approach allows the state to focus funds where it sees fit, but gives localities the discretion to use those funds in ways most relevant to local participants' needs. The nondiscretionary nature of EES's federal Comprehensive Child Development Program (CCDP) grant gives it the flexibility to meet the changing needs of its families and the community in which they live. Other states would do well to use the CCDP as a model for distributing grants.

Find new ways to invest in children's health.

The failure of the health care system to adequately serve the children in this country leaves states with little choice but to forge ahead on their own and attempt to address the inadequacies of the private and federal health care systems as best they can. Some of the options available to them are: improved funding for community health centers; more aggressive vaccination policies; the broadening of eligibility requirements for Medicaid and the expansion of its services covering young children; programs to enhance prenatal care and to reduce the incidence of teen pregnancy; increased state funding for the federal WIC program; and health insurance provided for children whose family incomes disqualify them from welfare or whose age places them outside the state limits for Medicaid coverage. State policies can also address the shortages of primary care physicians, especially in rural and inner-city areas, by providing incentives to doctors and medical schools.

Build the capacity for evaluation.

None of the three programs in our study has undertaken a full-scale evaluation of its entire range of activities. Instead, evaluation proceeds on a piecemeal basis, especially in cases where one or another of its components happens to be a research and demonstration project. Time and finances often act as barriers to evaluation. But, as states begin to meet the readiness goal, they will need to know how successful their efforts are in promoting child development and supporting families. Thus, it will be in their interest to allocate funds for program evaluations.

State-initiated evaluations should be flexible and allow local programs to examine the broad array of services they offer. They should make certain that the evaluation process minimizes paperwork, engages program participants and collaborating agencies, and is designed to be useful to the program staff. An evaluation that addresses questions of program implementation and the impact on participants of the program's provision of services will be useful to practitioners in shaping future program operations (Weiss and Halpern, 1990: 27 ff.). Such an evaluation can identify what works, what does not work, and why.

Recognizing that programs evolve over time and that success can be preceded by failure, states must assess program performance in phases and on realistic terms. Public officials, under pressure to obtain quick results, often focus solely on outcome evaluations in the early stages of program development. They would be well advised, instead, to heed the warning of noted sociologist Donald Campbell to avoid premature assessment and "evaluate no program until it is proud" (quoted in Weiss and Halpern, 1991: 32).

Provide assistance for staff training.

Staff training is crucial, but it can be expensive. In some geographic areas, quality training professionals are slim or nonexistent. Local programs will benefit greatly if the state can help with funds and resources for training. The paraprofessionals on whom most family support programs rely are in particular need of continuous training to compensate for gaps in their academic background. State agencies can design and purchase training materials and hire personnel to rotate throughout the state to local programs. Training conferences are particularly useful; staff members enjoy meeting their counterparts from other localities and brainstorming about common issues. Several of the federal funding programs that are distributed by state governments for child-related issues, including Child Care Improvement Grants, IV-A Risk Program, and Child Care Block Grants (Levy, Kagan, and Copple, 1992:12), can be used for training family support and child care staff.

The School as Home for Comprehensive Family Support

School-based early childhood and family support programs have the potential to achieve the readiness goal. Our research shows that *public schools can take the lead in creating a system of comprehensive early childhood services* that includes parenting education, family support, daycare, and health and social services. Among the strengths of the efforts undertaken by the three programs in this study to offer comprehensive services are:

- A flexible organization that allows staff to respond quickly to individual needs and to develop new programs for children and families;
- The mechanisms to ensure continuity despite changes in school leadership. These mechanisms include broad support from key school administrators and community members, staff development, and stable funding sources;
- The pooling of diverse resources (funds, space, personnel, time, training opportunities) to plan and implement a broad program for children and families; and

- The involvement of a range of community agencies to make multiple, as well as new, services convenient and accessible to families.

The readiness goal cannot be accomplished by schools alone, even if they take a lead role. Our research indicates that *meeting the goal requires a partnership of families, schools, and communities, and that this alliance must be built on the strengths of the partners.* "If you want to save the babies, make sure the mother has access to prenatal care, to immunizations, to knowledge of basic parenting skills, and to daycare that will allow her to continue her education to get a job," says Marion Wright Edelman of the Children's Defense Fund (Lewin, 1988:16). Parents do want to raise healthy children and, given the opportunity, will build on family strengths and work to further their own personal development. This is not to say that it will be an easy or quick process, especially for those who face serious challenges in their lives. The fact that the programs in our study reported low attrition and had waiting lists is a credit, not only to the programs, but to the participants themselves, who see these programs as enabling them to be the first and best teachers of their children.

Schools, aspiring to produce successful students, reach out to young children and their families. Most already have a staff of social workers, kindergarten teachers, special education teachers, and administrators with the training and experience to develop and manage comprehensive family support programs. Investing the responsibility for these programs in a semiautonomous unit within the school system is an effective strategy, as our case studies show. The unit is able to pull together a number of services and programs already offered by the school district. It works with community agencies to fill gaps in children's services and to coordinate more efficient service delivery. It has the flexibility to do what it takes to offer convenient, continuous, and comprehensive services.

The readiness goal highlights the importance and necessity of pooling community services for prevention and early intervention. Such preventive efforts begin with the knowledge of local resources and of ways to piece them together in a family-friendly way. Community agencies united for a common cause—children's well-being—can create the synergy to develop coordinated and preventive programming. Communities possess talent, creativity, and entrepreneurship. They have the services to achieve better outcomes for children and families. It is possible to muster the political will to bring about comprehensive family support, as our cases so ably demonstrate.

References

Alachua County Needs Assessment Committee and the United Way. (ND). *The path to our future*. Alachua County, FL: Author.

Bane, M. J. (1991). *Paying attention to children: Services, settings and systems*. A working paper of the Executive Session on Making the System Work for Poor Children. Cambridge, MA: Malcolm Wiener Center for Social Policy, John F. Kennedy School of Government, Harvard University.

Barr, D., & Cochran, M. (1992). Understanding and supporting empowerment: Redefining the professional role. *Networking Bulletin: Empowerment and Family Support*, 2(3), 1–8.

Benard, B. (1989). Working together: Principles of effective collaboration. *Prevention Forum*, 10(1), 71–79.

Boyer, E. L. (1991). *Ready to learn: A mandate for the nation*. Princeton, NJ: The Carnegie Foundation for the Advancement of Teaching.

Brattleboro Area Chamber of Commerce. (1992). *Brattleboro, Vermont*. Sarasota, FL: Chamber Publications of New England.

Bredekamp, S. (Ed.). (1992). *Developmentally appropriate practice in early childhood programs serving children from birth through age 8*. (Expanded edition.). Washington, DC: National Association for the Education of Young Children.

Bruner, C. (1991). *Thinking collaboratively: Ten questions and answers to help policymakers improve children's services*. Washington, DC: Education and Human Services Consortium.

Campbell, D. (1987). Problems for the experimenting society in the interface between evaluation and service providers. In S. L. Kagan, D. R. Powell, B. Weissbourd, & E. F. Zigler (Eds.), *America's family support programs: Perspectives and prospects*. New Haven, CT: Yale University Press.

Center for the Future of Children. (1992). Analysis. *The Future of Children*, 2(2), 7–24.

Cities in Schools, Inc. (1991). *The Cities in Schools program: Turning kids around.* Alexandria, VA: Author.

Coleman, J. S. (1987). Families and schools. *Educational Researcher,* 16(6), 32–38.

Coleman, J. S. (1991). *Policy perspectives: Parental involvement in education.* Washington, DC: U.S. Department of Education.

Colorado House Bill No. 1341. *An act concerning public education, and providing a new system for the financing thereof and making an appropriation in connection therewith.* Approved on May 24, 1988.

Council of Chief State School Officers. (1989). *Family support education and involvement: A guide for state action.* Washington, DC: Author.

Council of Chief State School Officers. (1992). *Student success through collaboration: A policy statement of the Council of Chief State School Officers.* Washington, DC: Author.

Dornbusch, S. M. & Wood, K. D. (1989). Family processes and educational achievement. In W. J. Weston (Ed.), *Education and the American family: A research synthesis.* New York, NY: New York University Press.

Farrow, F., & Joe, T. (1992). Financing school-linked, integrated services. *The Future of Children,* 2(1), 56–67.

Gamse, B. C., & Weiss, H. B. (1987). *What we know about home visits: A review of research and practice.* Cambridge, MA: Harvard Family Research Project.

Gross, J. F. (1991, Spring). On starting an in-home training program for family daycare providers. *Windham County Family Support Program Newsletter,* 5.

Harvard Family Research Project. (1993). *Building villages to raise our children: From programs to service systems.* Cambridge, MA: Author.

Kagan, S. L. (1990). Readiness 2000: Rethinking rhetoric and responsibility. *Phi Delta Kappan,* 72(4), 272–279.

Katz, L. G. (1992). Readiness: Children and schools. *ERIC Digest,* 2(1), 2–6.

Levy, J. E., Kagan, S. L., & Copple, C. (1992). *Are we ready? Collaboration to support young children and their families.* Washington, DC: American Public Welfare Association and Council of Chief State School Officers.

Lewin, T. (1988, March 8). Family support aims to mend two generations. *The New York Times,* A1, A12.

McCabe, J. R. (1992, March). *"The Center" project.* Unpublished manuscript.

National Association of State Boards of Education. (1991). *Caring communities: Supporting young children and families.* Alexandria, VA: Author.

National Commission on Children. (1991). *Beyond rhetoric: A new American agenda for children and families.* Washington, DC: Author.

National Governors' Association Action Team on School Readiness. (1992). *Benchmarks for educational success.* Washington, DC: National Governors' Association.

Powell, D. R. (1991). *Strengthening parental contributions to school readiness and early school learning.* Washington, DC: U.S. Department of Education.

Schorr, L. B. (1988). *Within our reach: Breaking the cycle of disadvantage.* New York, NY: Anchor Press/Doubleday.

Snow, C. E., Barnes, W. S., Chandler, J., Goodman, I. F., & Hemphill, L. (1991). *Unfulfilled expectations: Home and school influences on literacy.* Cambridge, MA: Harvard University Press.

U.S. Department of Education. (1991). *Preparing young children for success: Guideposts for achieving our first national goal.* Washington, DC: Author.

Weiss, H. B., & Halpern, R. (1990). *Community-based family support and education programs: Something old or something new?* New York, NY: National Center for Children in Poverty.

Weissbourd, B., & Kagan, S. L. (1989). Family support programs: Catalysts for change. *American Journal of Orthopsychiatry,* 59(1), 20–31.

Windham County Family Support Program. (1988). *Grant proposal submitted to the Comprehensive Child Development Program.* Brattleboro, VT: Author.

Windham County Family Support Program. (1992). *Beginnings: Parents and children learning together.* Brattleboro, VT: Brattleboro Town School District.

Windham County Family Support Program. (1993, April). [Data report]. Unpublished raw data.

Appendix I

Early Education Services

Brattleboro, Vermont

Early Education Services (EES) is an umbrella organization of the Brattleboro school district that develops, implements, and houses primary prevention and early intervention for families in Windham County, Vermont. These collaborative programs include Comprehensive Child Development Program (CCDP), Even Start, Parents As Teachers (PAT), Early Education Initiative, Follow Through, and Family School Partnership Program.

Origins

In 1987, in response to an alarming increase in the number of children who were not ready for school, the town of Brattleboro and the school district established a parent education program. The school district researched various school-based early intervention models and chose to implement a modified version of a home visiting program in Yakima, Washington. With seed capital from the town and a foundation, the school district began the program. This initial investment provided a basis for the program to secure grants to expand outreach and services.

Organization

EES is the early education unit of the Brattleboro town school district. Each of the EES subprograms has its own advisory board composed of parents and community members.

Agency Collaboration

Over the years EES has developed close working relationships with health, daycare, education, and human services providers in Brattleboro. EES makes and receives frequent referrals with these providers, attends interagency case conferences, and participates in joint service planning and coordination.

Goals

The programs run by EES strive to promote the healthy development of young children; prepare them to succeed in school; enhance the social, economic, and personal well-being of the whole family; and empower families to use existing community services more effectively.

Funding

EES services are countywide and are funded by local, state, and federal sources. The town of Brattleboro allocates $50,000 a year to support PAT. The Agency of Human Services, which funds the Parent-Child Center, allocated $25,000 in FY 1991-1992. Federal programs are funded yearly as follows: Even Start, $239,000; CCDP, $672,000; and Follow Through, $179,000. The federal programs require local matching funds and may increase funding in the coming years. The National Daycare Association also provides $200,000 for staff development for Follow Through. The total budget in FY 1992-1993 was $1.4 million.

Participants

The PAT program serves parents with children from birth to age four and pregnant women, regardless of income and education. The federal programs are targeted for specific populations and have well-defined eligibility criteria.

Staff

The staff for the different programs may include a combination of the following: home visitor, home tutor, nurse, early childhood educator, and social worker. All staff undergo regular, thorough, and extensive inservice training.

Services

The combined programs offer a wide array of services including home-based parent education; family literacy and adult education counseling; parent support groups; information resource and referral; health education, assessments, and support services; preschool; play groups; and child care information.

Parents' Role

Parents are represented in program advisory councils. As advisory board members, they participate in program development and fundraising, make budget and program recommendations, volunteer to help with program events, and provide community support for the program at town meetings.

Evaluation

The town of Brattleboro requires monitoring of the developmental progress of children in the PAT program. The federally funded programs—the CCDP, Follow Through, and Even Start—are being evaluated by independent evaluators with the help of program consultants.

Appendix II

The Center

Leadville, Colorado

The Center in Leadville Colorado, under the auspices of the school district, offers comprehensive child care and family support services to low-income, dual-earner parents. The Center provides quality daycare, preschool, and before- and afterschool programs 12 ½ hours a day, 365 days a year. It acts as a hub for community and social services.

Origins

When a large mine, the principal employer of the county closed down, Leadville experienced serious economic and social problems. Families that had once depended on the high unionized wages of one parent now found it necessary that both parents work—with the only option being low wage jobs at a considerable distance from Leadville. The Center was founded in 1987 by the school district in an attempt to address the need for quality daycare services as well as the growing local problems of school dropouts, teen pregnancies, latchkey children, and a lack of school readiness among children entering kindergarten.

Organization

The Center is administered by the Lake County School District, but operates as a nonprofit enterprise. Its board, composed of parents and community members, oversees the day-to-day operation of The Center.

Goals

The Center aims to be a true *center* of family support services for the Lake County area. It tries to provide dual-earner families with affordable, high quality care for their children. The Center hopes to expand its existing family services to develop a comprehensive "one stop shopping" network to better coordinate and simplify access to services and to provide individualized attention to families.

Agency Collaboration

Local and state organizations were involved in planning The Center; many of these have maintained their connections. For example, The Center has a referral agreement with the health department and works with officials there to coordinate children's health care.

Funding

The Center opened after the school district donated a vacant former elementary school and provided a $40,000 loan. It also obtained a $140,000 Community Development Block Grant, and $40,000 from Lake County. It now relies on tuition to provide 50 percent of its $600,000 budget (FY 1991–1992). The other 50 percent comes from a variety of sources: funds from the Department of Social Services to provide single-parent daycare; from Head Start to provide care for "at-risk" children; from the Mountain Valley Developmental Center; the State of Colorado Pilot Preschool Program; the Colorado Department of Education for preschool and handicapped children; and from a number of local and national foundations. Approximately 90 percent of the funding is continuous and lasting; foundation grants provide the last 10 percent.

Participants

The Center's programs are open to any family in Lake County. While some services are directed toward certain groups of people (e.g., single mothers), many are open to anyone who needs them. The fact that The Center is open to everybody is one reason for its success; because it is the hub of so many activities, there is no stigma attached to using any of its services.

Staff

The Center's staff comes from the community, and the majority was hired based on experience, expressions of warmth and nurturance, and dedication to working with children, rather than on academic qualifications. The Center provides extensive training and support for its staff. There are 33 teachers.

Services

The Center provides services to three groups of people: young children, adults, and teenagers. The Center works with many community agencies and volunteers to deliver its services.

Services for children consist of:

- a preschool program for children ages two-and-a-half to five
- a daycare program for children from infancy to age five
- a before- and afterschool program for children ages five to thirteen
- a Head Start program for sixty preschool children

Services for adults consist of:

- parent education classes
- GED and literacy classes
- Share Colorado food program
- child and family counseling through local service agencies

Services for teenagers consist of:

- prenatal education and care for young women and teenage girls
- a pregnancy prevention program
- vocational training in early childhood education for high school seniors
- parenting classes for all high school students

Parents' Role

Parents are encouraged to participate actively in The Center, but many are not able to do so because they work such long hours so far away. Thus The Center must find creative ways to involve parents. It holds many activities in the evenings and on weekends. Parents also serve on The Center's board of directors.

Evaluation

The Colorado Pilot Preschool Program conducts an assessment for the state-funded components. Program components funded by federal grants are evaluated separately.

Appendix III

Family Services Center

Gainesville, Florida

Operating from the premise that a child "cannot be educated in isolation of her or his family," the Family Services Center provides family support, early childhood and adult education, health, and social services in a school-based setting. Founded by the School Board of Alachua County and the Florida Department of Health and Rehabilitative Services, the Family Services Center maintains strong ties to both, and remains a school-based program, housed in seven mobile units. The Family Services Center is an arm of the school board and is linked formally through representative guidance counselors to middle and elementary schools.

Origins

Established in August 1990, the Family Services Center is a response to community leaders' concerns about poverty in Gainesville and its impact on children's school performance. While Gainesville, the seat of Alachua county, is a university town with several major hospitals and a visible professional community, many parts of the city are poor. Due to the reality of so many children living in poverty, the Gainesville school district and community agencies sought to provide comprehensive services to families in a convenient and accessible manner.

Organization

The Family Services Center operates as a unit of the school board. It is directed by a school principal, and falls within the division of early childhood services, which has purview over all preschool programs including Head Start.

Goals

The goals of the Family Services Center are two-fold. First, the Family Services Center assists families in improving their children's school performance. Second, the program focuses on a family's total needs through coordination of on-site and off-site services.

Agency Collaboration

The planning necessary to co-locate health, education, economic, and social services at one school site meant that the agencies involved in the Family Services Center had to clarify their roles, and that planners had to recognize their interdependence. Although the school board took the lead in collaborating with the Department of Health and Rehabilitative Services, it acknowledged the need for community involvement as well. Today, the key agencies collaborating with the Family Services Center are the University of Florida, Santa Fe Community College, various community and social service agencies, and city and county government.

Funding

To fund their $1 million budget, the Family Services Center employs a diverse funding and resource strategy that includes the following components: (1) redirection of existing funds from community agencies that reassign their staff to the Family Services Center; (2) federal school funds such as Chapter 1 and Chapter 2; (3) grants from state and federal programs; (4) federal entitlements such as Medicaid; and (5) in-kind contributions and volunteers from the community. The Family Services Center has also received a grant of $2.5 million from the Public Education Capital Outlay Fund, a fund governed by the Florida State Department of Education.

Participants

"At-risk" students and needy families who qualify for health and social services are referred by school personnel to the Family Services Center. The Family Services Center provides services to students enrolled in 28 schools. Currently, about 400 families participate. Health services are also open to members of the community who are eligible for Medicaid.

Staff

The staffs come from diverse backgrounds and include teachers, teaching aides, parent educators, social workers, nurses, psychologists, and administrative assistants. There are both full-time and part-time staff members. Some are reassigned from community agencies to work at the Family Services Center.

Services

Services are comprehensive and include health care, early childhood education, adult education, parenting skills, family counseling, and employment assistance to families who qualify for them.

- Health and mental health services, provided through the state-funded Supplemental School Health Program and the Full Service School, and by the Public Health Department, include a clinic available to program participants and Medicaid-eligible families.
- Family support services, provided through the Chapter 2 Parenting Program and the Head Start Family Services Center Demonstration Project, include parenting discussions, support groups, and social and recreation activities.
- Vocational education, adult education, and career counseling—provided by the Even Start Family Literacy Program, the Head Start Family Services Center Demonstration Project, and the Family Services Center Computer Lab—include GED classes and a chance to learn computer skills.
- Economic and social services are provided through the Florida Department of Health and Rehabilitative Services.
- Developmental services for children, provided by Florida First Start, include educational activities for children ages birth to three and their parents. Parent educators make monthly home visits to teach parents how to provide stimulating activities for their children.

Parents' Role

The Family Services Center encourages parents to be teachers as well as advocates for their children. In addition to teaching parents about early childhood development, the Family Services Center's various programs work to help the parents meet their own education, vocational, and parenting goals.

Evaluation

Federal components of the program, such as Even Start, are independently evaluated.

Appendix IV

Research Methods and Data Analysis

Identifying and Choosing Programs

The initial phase of our research consisted of defining the criteria for selecting program sites. We looked for programs that were school-affiliated; offered comprehensive education, health, family support, and social services; benefited parents as well as children; promoted parent involvement; served participants for at least two years of the child's life; and involved community-based collaborations. Through calls to key informants and a review of the family support literature, we requested program information either by telephone or letter to over 50 state and local programs. We received information ranging from public relations brochures to extensive materials that included legislation, grant proposals, and annual reports. Based on a careful document review of approximately 30 programs, we culled the most promising ones. Follow-up phone calls with program directors completed our initial round of information gathering. From these procedures we chose our program sites.

Research Instruments

We prepared different sets of interview schedules to match the categories of informants to be included in our study: program directors, staff, school officials, community agency representatives, and parents. Our questions were open-ended; some were general, others were tailored to the specific characteristics of a program. Senior Harvard Family Research Project (HFRP) staff members reviewed the instruments and gave their comments. Our first field site also served to pretest the instruments.

Field Research

Field research for each site took at least a month of preparation. We worked with the program director to determine a suitable time to visit and informed her that we wanted to interview different informants. Because of time and resource constraints, we did not have the opportunity to select parents for our focus groups. Instead, we asked the program director to invite parents who represented the range of participants in a program. Many minute details had to be worked out by the program director—for which we are thankful—including a space where we could hold our interviews, and refreshments and child care during our focus groups with parents.

Our field research for each site involved a three- to five-day visit by a team of two or three researchers. On average, we conducted twelve in-depth interviews and two focus groups, one with parents and another with staff. All these sessions were tape recorded. We also collected additional documentation, joined home visits, participated in parenting sessions, and observed child care facilities and preschool classrooms. Inevitably, we got to know more about the neighborhoods and communities where families lived and children grew up.

A typical field schedule looked like this:

Day 1	a.m.	Arrival
	p.m.	Interview program director
Day 2	a.m.	Interview school Hold focus group with parents Interview one of the program's coordinators
	p.m.	Interview staff early childhood specialist Hold first staff focus group Dinner with program director
Day 3	a.m.	Interview program's social worker Interview director of mental health services Observe home visit
	p.m.	Interview director of health department Interview director of employment and training Interview kindergarten teacher Dinner with program evaluator
Day 4	a.m.	Hold second staff focus group Interview program's former director Attend parenting session
	p.m.	Interview elementary school principal Interview one of the program's coordinators
Day 5	a.m.	Visit child care center Visit preschool

Organizing Data

Our taped interviews were transcribed at the HFRP office. The transcribed interviews were then coded on Ethnograph software. This system allowed us to organize and compare qualitative data—based on codes such as staff training, program eligibility, and ease of collaboration—within a program and across programs. Altogether we developed 40 coded categories.

Report Writing

There were three stages to the writing process. First, we summarized the information on each program based on documents, field notes, and the Ethnograph printouts. This was followed by writing the different sections of this report using the summaries. We then sent out drafts of the report for review and comment and in the final stage, revised and edited the manuscript.

About the Harvard Family Research Project

The Harvard Family Research Project was established in 1983 at the Harvard Graduate School of Education by Dr. Heather B. Weiss, who continues as its director. The project conducts and disseminates research about programs and policies to strengthen and support families with young children.

The project's mission is to examine and assist in the development of policies and programs to empower families and communities as contexts of human development.

Specializing in applied policy research, the project's outlook encompasses the view that to educate the whole child, parents, schools, and other community agencies must redefine their roles to include partnerships to support child development from infancy through adolescence. It maintains that to sustain gains, support initiatives must be continuous over a child's life.

The project is nationally recognized for providing much of the data demonstrating the value of preventive, comprehensive, collaborative, and family-focused services. It has a diverse research agenda, supported by public and private funders, that is designed to inform and shape national policy debates, advance evaluation practice, and encourage progressive program development.

The audience for the project's work ranges from national and state policy makers to researchers and local practitioners, many of whom have benefited from the project's ability to provide new perspectives and suggest creative solutions.